Jet Set JUMBLE®

A Wealth of Puzzles to Enrich Your Mind

Henri Arnold, Bob Lee, and Mike Argirion

TRIUMPH
BOOKS

Jumble® is a registered trademark
of Tribune Media Services, Inc.

Triumph Books and colophon are registered trademarks of
Random House, Inc.

This book is available in quantity at special discounts
for your group or organization.

For further information, contact:

Triumph Books
542 South Dearborn Street
Suite 750
Chicago, Illinois 60605
(312) 939-3330
Fax (312) 663-3557
www.triumphbooks.com

Printed in U.S.A.

ISBN: 978-1-60078-353-1

Design by Sue Knopf

CONTENTS

Jet Set
JUMBLE®

Classic
Puzzles

JUMBLE®

Unscramble these four Jumbles, one letter to each square, to form four ordinary words.

YENAH

POLEE

REFOLG

TUCLED

They're on their honeymoon

WHAT THE SWIM-
MERS TOOK
WHEN THEY GOT
MARRIED.

Now arrange the circled letters to form the surprise answer, as suggested by the above cartoon.

Print answer here ◯◯◯ " ◯◯◯◯◯◯◯ "

JUMBLE®

Unscramble these four Jumbles, one letter to each square, to form four ordinary words.

TAUCE

ANDAP

ROMMEY

SCETOK

My makeup is all wrong, and you're not shooting my good side

WHAT THE OBNOXIOUS ACTRESS DID ON THE SET.

Now arrange the circled letters to form the surprise answer, as suggested by the above cartoon.

Print answer here ◯◯◯◯ A " ◯◯◯◯◯ "

JUMBLE®

Unscramble these four Jumbles, one letter to each square, to form four ordinary words.

TIFAN

ARBIN

YARFER

GROUTH

Go wash up. I'll get your meal ready right now

I'm hungry

WHERE MOM PUT DINNER WHEN SHE GOT HOME LATE.

Now arrange the circled letters to form the surprise answer, as suggested by the above cartoon.

Print answer here ON THE ☐☐☐☐☐ ☐☐☐☐☐☐

JUMBLE®

Unscramble these four Jumbles, one letter to each square, to form four ordinary words.

MOBUX

YIRAH

BEBJOR

HINTEZ

They have a lovely sound

WHAT THE NON-DENOMINATIONAL CHOIR PRODUCED.

Now arrange the circled letters to form the surprise answer, as suggested by the above cartoon.

Print answer here " ◯◯◯◯◯◯◯ "

JUMBLE®

Unscramble these four Jumbles, one letter to each square, to form four ordinary words.

HUMOT

FYNAC

REDGUT

STOLCY

My old one wore out. Wouldn't add

THE ACCOUNTANT BOUGHT A NEW CALCULATOR SO HE---

Now arrange the circled letters to form the surprise answer, as suggested by the above cartoon.

Print answer here

" " ON IT

JUMBLE®

Unscramble these four Jumbles, one letter to
each square, to form four ordinary words.

GADMO

HICED

TEOGUN

SWEEFT

Only two dozen? I could
gather more myself

WHAT THE CHICKEN
FARMER DID TO
HIS WORKERS.

Now arrange the circled letters to form the
surprise answer, as suggested by the above
cartoon.

Print
answer
here   " ◯◯◯◯◯ " ◯◯◯◯ ON

JUMBLE®

Unscramble these four Jumbles, one letter to each square, to form four ordinary words.

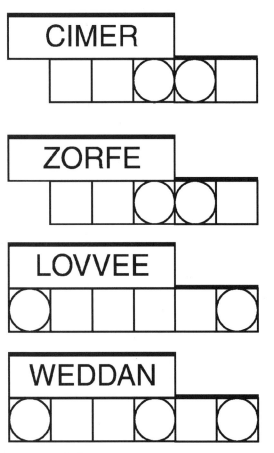

CIMER

ZORFE

LOVVEE

WEDDAN

I used to get 12 for 10 cents

10¢

WHEN GRANDPA BOUGHT GUMBALLS, THEY WERE----

Now arrange the circled letters to form the surprise answer, as suggested by the above cartoon.

Print answer here A ⬡⬡⬡⬡ A ⬡⬡⬡⬡⬡⬡

JUMBLE®

Unscramble these four Jumbles, one letter to each square, to form four ordinary words.

LUKKS

DATUC

DYFLON

CAFEDE

10 below right now. No relief in sight

I need another sweater

WHAT THE WEATHERMAN GAVE THE LISTENERS.

Now arrange the circled letters to form the surprise answer, as suggested by the above cartoon.

Print answer here THE "⬚⬚⬚⬚" ⬚⬚⬚⬚⬚

JUMBLE®

Unscramble these four Jumbles, one letter to
each square, to form four ordinary words.

YOGGS

TRUIF

DULCED

EBONGE

Is he married?

I don't
see a
ring

WHEN THE
WOMAN SPOTTED
THE HANDSOME
BACHELOR, HE
WAS---

Now arrange the circled letters to form the
surprise answer, as suggested by the above
cartoon.

Print
answer
here   " ⬡⬡⬡⬡⬡⬡⬡ " ⬡⬡⬡

JUMBLE®

Unscramble these four Jumbles, one letter to
each square, to form four ordinary words.

SUHOE

HOTOB

HYRITT

GLEZUZ

I need a mower,
not a club

WHEN THE GOLFER
ENDED UP IN THE
TALL GRASS, HE
SAID, "THIS IS ———"

Now arrange the circled letters to form the
surprise answer, as suggested by the above
cartoon.

*Print
answer* A
here

JUMBLE®

Unscramble these four Jumbles, one letter to each square, to form four ordinary words.

YOLID

HERIK

AXALGY

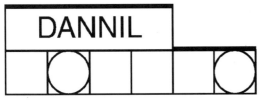

DANNIL

Faster!

WHEN THE KIDS
WANTED A RIDE
IN THE WAGON,
DAD----

Now arrange the circled letters to form the surprise answer, as suggested by the above cartoon.

Print answer here  " " IT

JUMBLE®

Unscramble these four Jumbles, one letter to
each square, to form four ordinary words.

FOTOA

YAGUD

RUZZEB

YECKAL

Now you look
like a monarch

WHAT A "LARGE"
CHANGE MADE
THE KING----

Now arrange the circled letters to form the
surprise answer, as suggested by the above
cartoon.

Print answer here " ⬡⬡⬡⬡⬡ "

JUMBLE®

Unscramble these four Jumbles, one letter to each square, to form four ordinary words.

ZOTAP

PRIVE

NERCRO

GIRDIF

One thousand dollars goes to 40526

That's me!

WHAT SHE WON AT THE RAFFLE.

Now arrange the circled letters to form the surprise answer, as suggested by the above cartoon.

Print answer here   THE "⃝⃝⃝⃝⃝" ⃝⃝⃝⃝⃝⃝

JUMBLE®

Unscramble these four Jumbles, one letter to
each square, to form four ordinary words.

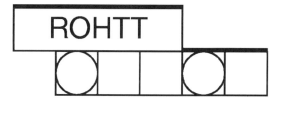

ROHTT

SYNAP

FLOUBE

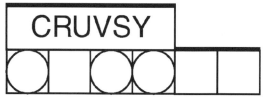

CRUVSY

They
didn't
like
the
food

EXPERIENCED BY
THE CHEF WHEN
THE DINERS
RETURNED THE
MEALS.

Now arrange the circled letters to form the
surprise answer, as suggested by the above
cartoon.

Print
answer
here

A

JUMBLE®

Unscramble these four Jumbles, one letter to
each square, to form four ordinary words.

BLEER

THEFC

JYLFOU

ETSAUL

You'd make a
lovely portrait.
May I buy you
a drink?

Beat it,
Buster

WHAT SHE GAVE
THE ARTIST ON
THE PROWL.

Now arrange the circled letters to form the
surprise answer, as suggested by the above
cartoon.

Print answer here THE ⬭⬭⬭⬭⬭-⬭⬭⬭

JUMBLE®

Unscramble these four Jumbles, one letter to each square, to form four ordinary words.

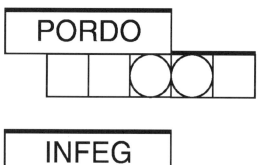

PORDO

INFEG

GREBID

PECTOK

This one sends me

Right on, sir

THE BANJO PLAYER SELECTED THE NEW CAR BECAUSE HE WAS----

Now arrange the circled letters to form the surprise answer, as suggested by the above cartoon.

Print answer here

 AT "  "

JUMBLE®

Unscramble these four Jumbles, one letter to each square, to form four ordinary words.

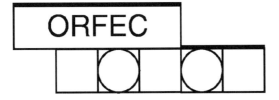
ORFEC

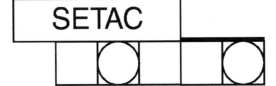
SETAC

ALCIME

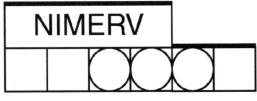
NIMERV

Ahhh! Just me and the wild blue yonder

EAT AT JOE'S

WHAT HE FLEW WHEN HE GOT HIS PILOT'S LICENSE.

Now arrange the circled letters to form the surprise answer, as suggested by the above cartoon.

Print answer here

" ◯◯◯◯◯◯◯◯◯◯ "

JUMBLE®

Unscramble these four Jumbles, one letter to each square, to form four ordinary words.

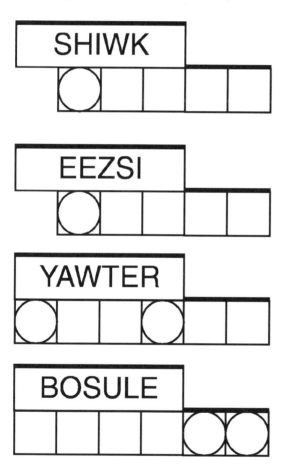

SHIWK

EEZSI

YAWTER

BOSULE

Wonderful for your first try, darling

WHEN SHE MADE HER OWN DRESS, MOM SAID IT WAS----

Now arrange the circled letters to form the surprise answer, as suggested by the above cartoon.

Print answer here

JUMBLE®

Unscramble these four Jumbles, one letter to each square, to form four ordinary words.

LALAM

GUBEN

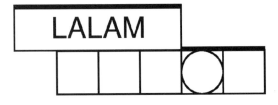

GONALO

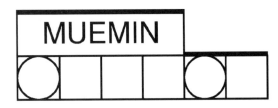

MUEMIN

It's like this every year

ORDERS

HOW HE DESCRIBED HIS FIREWORKS BUSINESS.

Now arrange the circled letters to form the surprise answer, as suggested by the above cartoon.

Print answer here " ◯◯◯◯◯◯◯◯ "

JUMBLE

Unscramble these four Jumbles, one letter to each square, to form four ordinary words.

KERAM

TURBS

PREEWT

TONKYT

As soon as I doze off it wakes me up

PLINK!

WHAT THE INTER-ROGATOR EXPERI-ENCED WHEN THE FAUCET DRIPPED ALL NIGHT.

Now arrange the circled letters to form the surprise answer, as suggested by the above cartoon.

Print answer here

JUMBLE®

Unscramble these four Jumbles, one letter to each square, to form four ordinary words.

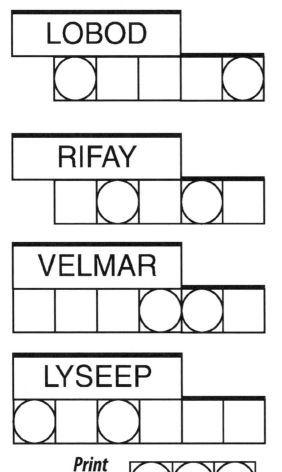

LOBOD

RIFAY

VELMAR

LYSEEP

... And the mist enveloped their love ...

Now you're getting it, Priscilla

WHEN THE POETRY STUDENT'S WORK IMPROVED, SHE WENT FROM---

Now arrange the circled letters to form the surprise answer, as suggested by the above cartoon.

Print answer here

TO " "

JUMBLE®

Unscramble these four Jumbles, one letter to each square, to form four ordinary words.

VALIA

SVORI

COBEME

CILOPY

I'm here in four...er...three

WHAT THE SHADY GOLFER TRIED TO DO.

Now arrange the circled letters to form the surprise answer, as suggested by the above cartoon.

Print answer here

☐☐☐☐☐☐☐ HIS " ☐☐☐ "

JUMBLE®

Unscramble these four Jumbles, one letter to
each square, to form four ordinary words.

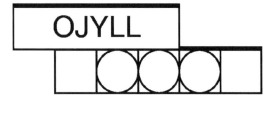

OJYLL

SHOWE

YAARTS

WINDAR

30 hot dogs. The winner!

Where does
he put it?

WHEN THE SKINNY
GUY WON THE
EATING CONTEST,
HIS COMPETITORS
FOUND IT----

Now arrange the circled letters to form the
surprise answer, as suggested by the above
cartoon.

**Print
answer
here**

TO " "

JUMBLE®

Unscramble these four Jumbles, one letter to each square, to form four ordinary words.

AYLIG

RYMEE

FALLUW

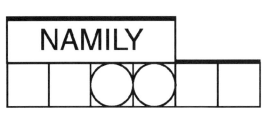

NAMILY

Thanks. You're so big and strong

May I call you?

WHAT SHE GOT FROM THE COL-LEGE JOCK IN THE LAUNDRY ROOM.

Now arrange the circled letters to form the surprise answer, as suggested by the above cartoon.

Print answer here A

JUMBLE®

Unscramble these four Jumbles, one letter to each square, to form four ordinary words.

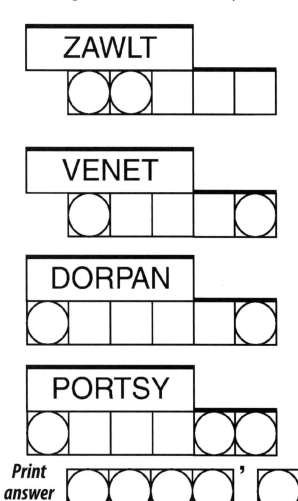

ZAWLT

VENET

DORPAN

PORTSY

How about a pizza tonight, Clara?

I only go to the finest places

PRINT SHOP

SHE SPURNED THE PRINTER'S ADVANCES BECAUSE HE‑‑‑

Now arrange the circled letters to form the surprise answer, as suggested by the above cartoon.

Print answer here ○○○○ ' ○ HER " ○○○○ "

Jet Set JUMBLE®

Daily Puzzles

JUMBLE®

Unscramble these four Jumbles, one letter to
each square, to form four ordinary words.

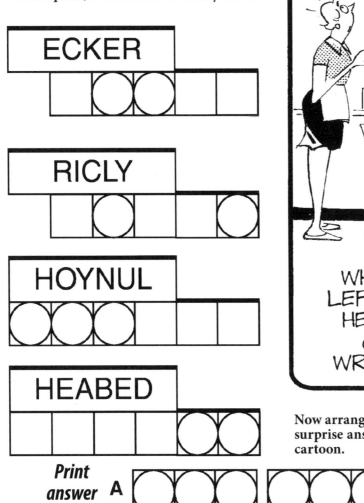

ECKER

RICLY

HOYNUL

HEABED

That's not
blond — *EEK!*

WHAT SHE WAS
LEFT WITH WHEN
HER HAIR CAME
OUT THE
WRONG COLOR.

Now arrange the circled letters to form the
surprise answer, as suggested by the above
cartoon.

*Print
answer
here*

28

JUMBLE.

Unscramble these four Jumbles, one letter to each square, to form four ordinary words.

ERRAM

GERME

LUSHIM

SUPCAM

104 today and tomorrow, with no relief in sight

THE FORECASTER DESCRIBED THE HEAT WAVE AS----

Now arrange the circled letters to form the surprise answer, as suggested by the above cartoon.

Print answer here

A

JUMBLE®

Unscramble these four Jumbles, one letter to
each square, to form four ordinary words.

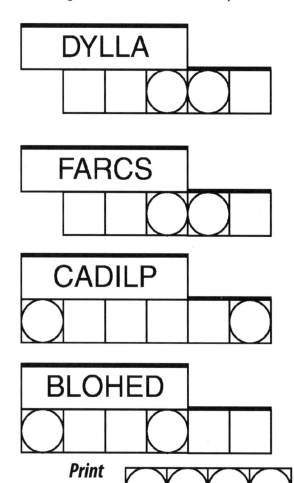

DYLLA

FARCS

CADILP

BLOHED

Should auld
acquaintance...

HAPPY
NEW
YEAR

THE ONLY TIME OF
YEAR THE CROWD
WANTED THE STAR
SHORTSTOP TO
DO THIS.

Now arrange the circled letters to form the
surprise answer, as suggested by the above
cartoon.

**Print
answer
here**

THE " "

JUMBLE

Unscramble these four Jumbles, one letter to
each square, to form four ordinary words.

SYTTA

VALIT

TEWGIN

DICHOR

I think this will
defrost in no time

I'm hungry

WHAT IT TAKES TO
MAKE A FAST MEAL.

Now arrange the circled letters to form the
surprise answer, as suggested by the above
cartoon.

**Print
answer
here**

OF " "

JUMBLE®

Unscramble these four Jumbles, one letter to each square, to form four ordinary words.

LAIDY

LEHEW

LIPOCE

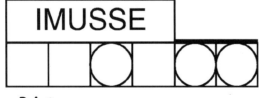

IMUSSE

This isn't marble. You're nothing but a cheat

WHY THE MOGUL DIDN'T PAY THE SCULPTOR FOR THE BUST.

Now arrange the circled letters to form the surprise answer, as suggested by the above cartoon.

Print answer here HE ◯◯◯ " ◯◯◯◯◯◯◯◯ "

JUMBLE®

Unscramble these four Jumbles, one letter to each square, to form four ordinary words.

GOBUM

YUNNF

RANBEN

RUMAID

Here's $75 in quarters. You count it!

COLLECTOR

WHAT THE ANGRY DRIVER USED TO PAY HIS SPEEDING FINE.

Now arrange the circled letters to form the surprise answer, as suggested by the above cartoon.

Print answer here " ◯◯◯ " ◯◯◯◯◯

JUMBLE®

Unscramble these four Jumbles, one letter to each square, to form four ordinary words.

ALTEM

URUGA

FLOSSI

LALPAP

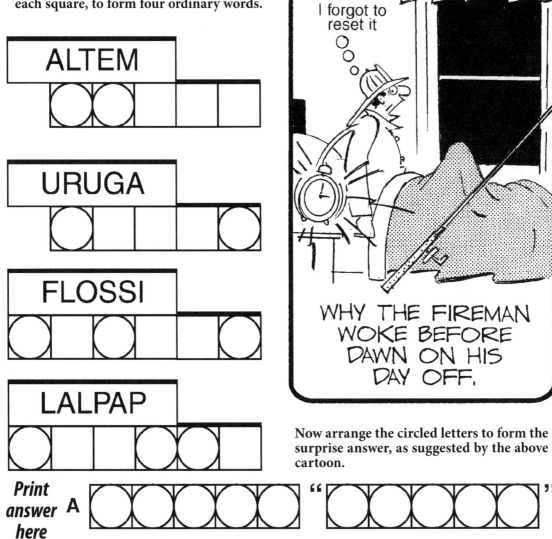

I forgot to reset it

WHY THE FIREMAN WOKE BEFORE DAWN ON HIS DAY OFF.

Now arrange the circled letters to form the surprise answer, as suggested by the above cartoon.

Print answer here

A ⬡⬡⬡⬡⬡ "⬡⬡⬡⬡⬡"

JUMBLE®

Unscramble these four Jumbles, one letter to
each square, to form four ordinary words.

NUWDE

LOFAR

TILPUF

TRABEN

This will satisfy
your needs

He has 20
years
experience

Very
personable

THE FURNITURE
SALESMAN WAS
HIRED BECAUSE
HE WAS---

Now arrange the circled letters to form the
surprise answer, as suggested by the above
cartoon.

Print
answer
here

" "

JUMBLE®

Unscramble these four Jumbles, one letter to each square, to form four ordinary words.

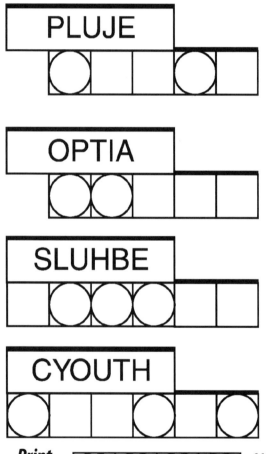

PLUJE

OPTIA

SLUHBE

CYOUTH

Delicious, Loretta

I have my dear grandmother to thank

HOW SHE FELT WHEN HER COBBLER RECIPE WON THE BLUE RIBBON.

Now arrange the circled letters to form the surprise answer, as suggested by the above cartoon.

Print answer here ◯◯◯◯ "◯◯◯◯◯◯◯"

JUMBLE®

Unscramble these four Jumbles, one letter to
each square, to form four ordinary words.

BOINS

HIWSS

TANNIE

GLUBIN

Let's go! I can't do everything myself!

Slave driver

WHEN THE KITCHEN HELP FELL BEHIND, THE CHEF WAS----

Now arrange the circled letters to form the
surprise answer, as suggested by the above
cartoon.

Print answer here "⬡⬡⬡⬡⬡⬡⬡"

JUMBLE®

Unscramble these four Jumbles, one letter to
each square, to form four ordinary words.

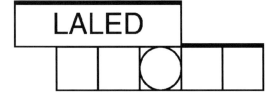
LALED

BYBOH

CASMIO

DOLIBY

You've been on
your knees
all day

Corn needs
lots of water
and sun

HARD TO RAISE
AFTER SPRING
PLANTING.

Now arrange the circled letters to form the
surprise answer, as suggested by the above
cartoon.

Print answer here

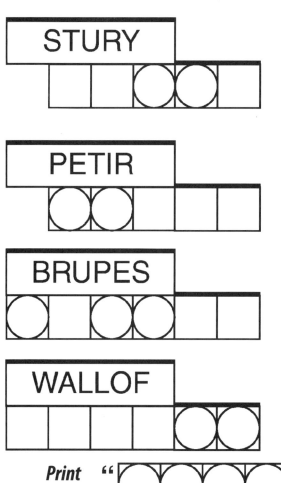

JUMBLE®

Unscramble these four Jumbles, one letter to
each square, to form four ordinary words.

STURY

PETIR

BRUPES

WALLOF

Stop, thief!

POLICE!!

WHEN HER PURSE
WAS SNATCHED,
THE TURNPIKE
OASIS BECAME A---

Now arrange the circled letters to form the
surprise answer, as suggested by the above
cartoon.

 *Print
answer
here*

JUMBLE.

Unscramble these four Jumbles, one letter to
each square, to form four ordinary words.

RINED

BICCU

BOAMEA

MERCOH

Yesterday I found
a nice bracelet

WHAT THE BARBER
DID ON VACATION.

Now arrange the circled letters to form the
surprise answer, as suggested by the above
cartoon.

**Print
answer
here**   "⬡⬡⬡⬡⬡⬡" THE ⬡⬡⬡⬡⬡

40

JUMBLE®

Unscramble these four Jumbles, one letter to
each square, to form four ordinary words.

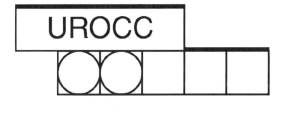

UROCC

SBELS

SNULES

ARIVED

I'm getting my degree
this year. Forty years
late

WHEN THE RETIREE
RETURNED TO
COLLEGE, HE WAS
PLACED IN THE---

Now arrange the circled letters to form the
surprise answer, as suggested by the above
cartoon.

Print
answer
here

" ⬡⬡⬡⬡⬡⬡ "   ⬡⬡⬡⬡⬡

JUMBLE®

Unscramble these four Jumbles, one letter to each square, to form four ordinary words.

EXIDO

CASEE

UPVERY

REVOUD

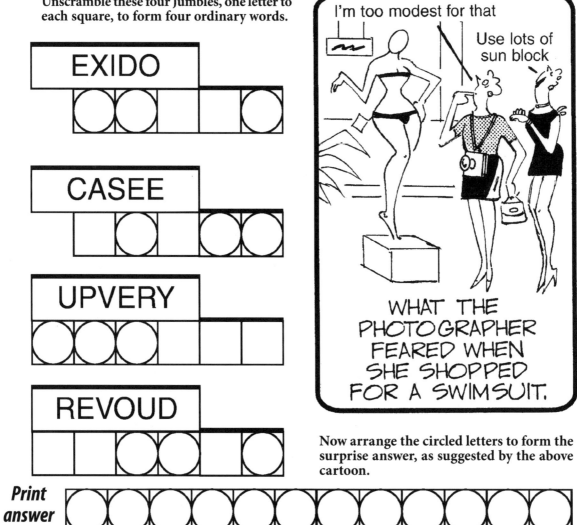

I'm too modest for that

Use lots of sun block

WHAT THE PHOTOGRAPHER FEARED WHEN SHE SHOPPED FOR A SWIMSUIT.

Now arrange the circled letters to form the surprise answer, as suggested by the above cartoon.

Print answer here

JUMBLE®

Unscramble these four Jumbles, one letter to each square, to form four ordinary words.

CEEPI

MUSIN

TANGOU

HINSAB

I hear Helen caught her boyfriend...

THIS CAN CURL YOUR HAIR AT A BEAUTY SALON.

Now arrange the circled letters to form the surprise answer, as suggested by the above cartoon.

Print answer here

JUMBLE®

Unscramble these four Jumbles, one letter to each square, to form four ordinary words.

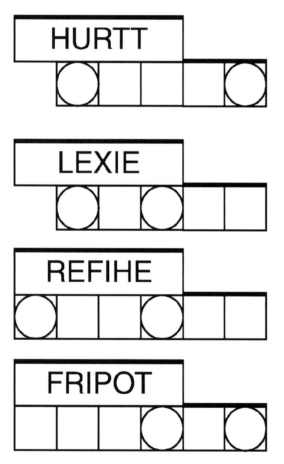

HURTT

LEXIE

REFIHE

FRIPOT

IN WHAT INNING DID THEY PASS THE BOTTLE AROUND?

Now arrange the circled letters to form the surprise answer, as suggested by the above cartoon.

Print answer here ◯◯◯ " ◯◯◯◯◯ "

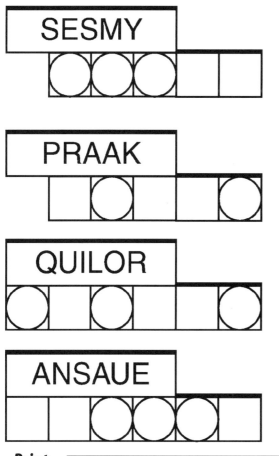

JUMBLE®

Unscramble these four Jumbles, one letter to each square, to form four ordinary words.

SESMY

PRAAK

QUILOR

ANSAUE

Pass the potatoes and more gravy, please

A ROUND BELLY CAN BE THE RESULT OF TOO MANY----

Now arrange the circled letters to form the surprise answer, as suggested by the above cartoon.

Print answer here

JUMBLE®

Unscramble these four Jumbles, one letter to
each square, to form four ordinary words.

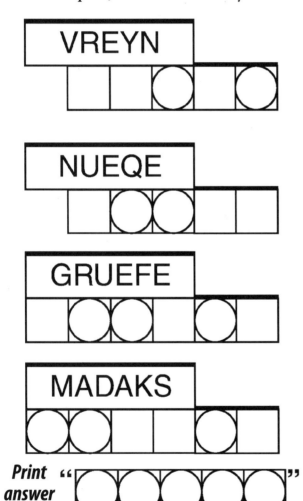

VREYN

NUEQE

GRUEFE

MADAKS

**Print
answer
here**
" ◯◯◯◯◯ " THE ◯◯◯◯◯

All I want on it is
"Happy Birthday, Sally"

What kind
of frosting?

WHAT SHE TOLD
THE BAKER TO
DO ON HER
BIRTHDAY CAKE.

Now arrange the circled letters to form the
surprise answer, as suggested by the above
cartoon.

JUMBLE®

Unscramble these four Jumbles, one letter to
each square, to form four ordinary words.

WEFER

YEVAH

DYSTUR

YIFFEG

Full academic
scholarship

Thanks,
Dad

SHE WENT AWAY
TO COLLEGE IN
A NEW CAR
BECAUSE SHE----

Now arrange the circled letters to form the
surprise answer, as suggested by the above
cartoon.

Print
answer
here

" "

JUMBLE®

Unscramble these four Jumbles, one letter to each square, to form four ordinary words.

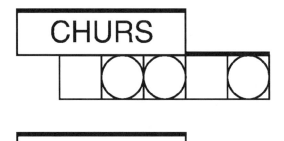

CHURS

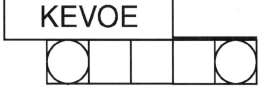

KEVOE

TABBIR

POLEEP

I told you it was a piece of junk

WHEN HE BOUGHT THE JALOPY, HE ENDED UP WITH A---

Now arrange the circled letters to form the surprise answer, as suggested by the above cartoon.

Print answer here

 OF

JUMBLE®

Unscramble these four Jumbles, one letter to each square, to form four ordinary words.

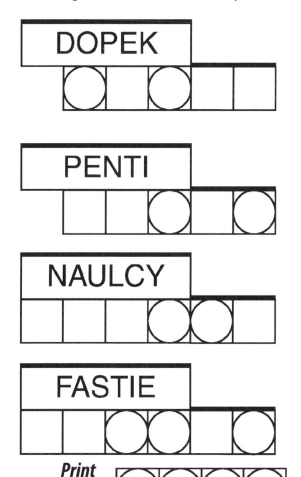

DOPEK

PENTI

NAULCY

FASTIE

Your test score is not encouraging

Whatever

AN INDIFFERENT STUDENT CAN DO THIS IN ASTRON- OMY CLASS.

Now arrange the circled letters to form the surprise answer, as suggested by the above cartoon.

Print answer here

UP " "

49

JUMBLE®

Unscramble these four Jumbles, one letter to each square, to form four ordinary words.

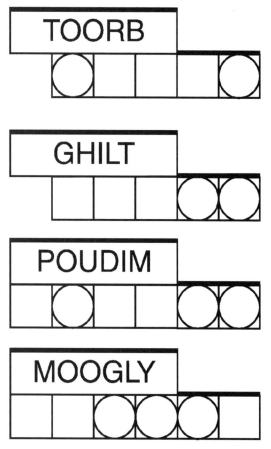

TOORB

GHILT

POUDIM

MOOGLY

WHAT THE FAST-TALKING MECHANIC SEEMED TO BE---

Now arrange the circled letters to form the surprise answer, as suggested by the above cartoon.

Print answer here A " ◯◯◯◯◯◯ " ◯◯◯◯◯◯

JUMBLE®

Unscramble these four Jumbles, one letter to each square, to form four ordinary words.

GLOIN

DEPIT

REGEME

WUCREF

Let's go

That looks dangerous. I'm out

WHY HE DIDN'T JOIN THE GLACIER EXPEDITION.

Now arrange the circled letters to form the surprise answer, as suggested by the above cartoon.

Print answer here HE GOT " ⬡⬡⬡⬡ " ⬡⬡⬡⬡

JUMBLE®

Unscramble these four Jumbles, one letter to
each square, to form four ordinary words.

GEALL

GNAAP

DAILIN

AREETA

It's been 50 years.
Let's stay in touch

NORTH-
SOUTH
HIGH
REUNION

THE BALD-HEADED
FRIENDS HAD A
DIFFICULT TIME
DOING THIS.

Now arrange the circled letters to form the
surprise answer, as suggested by the above
cartoon.

Print answer here " ◯◯◯◯◯◯◯ "

JUMBLE®

Unscramble these four Jumbles, one letter to
each square, to form four ordinary words.

CINEW

DEGEH

URKEEB

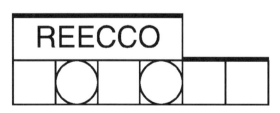
REECCO

What's it going to be?

Shhh! This takes concentration

KNITTED WITH A COMPLEX STITCH.

Now arrange the circled letters to form the
surprise answer, as suggested by the above
cartoon.

Print answer here

JUMBLE®

Unscramble these four Jumbles, one letter to
each square, to form four ordinary words.

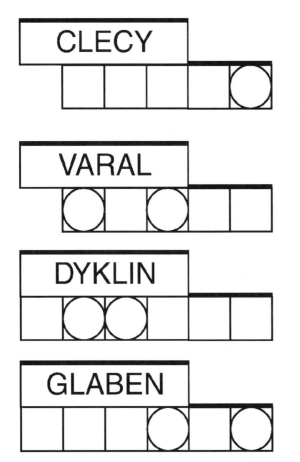

CLECY

VARAL

DYKLIN

GLABEN

I'm exhausted,
but I won't
give up

AFTER AN HOUR-
LONG BATTLE WITH
THE MARLIN, THE
FISHERMAN WAS----

Now arrange the circled letters to form the
surprise answer, as suggested by the above
cartoon.

Print answer here "⬡⬡⬡⬡⬡⬡⬡⬡"

JUMBLE®

Unscramble these four Jumbles, one letter to each square, to form four ordinary words.

WOGAL

DEGAL

MOANAZ

KOYDEN

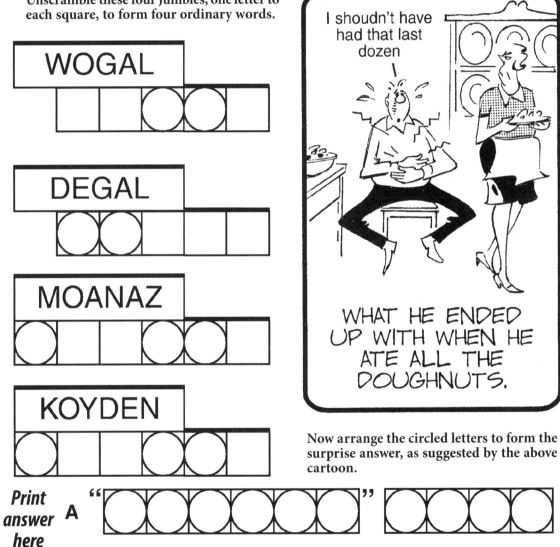

I shoudn't have had that last dozen

WHAT HE ENDED UP WITH WHEN HE ATE ALL THE DOUGHNUTS.

Now arrange the circled letters to form the surprise answer, as suggested by the above cartoon.

Print answer here

A " ⬡⬡⬡⬡⬡⬡ " ⬡⬡⬡⬡

JUMBLE®

Unscramble these four Jumbles, one letter to each square, to form four ordinary words.

RACHI

TELLU

RUFLYR

YUIRPT

...And it turned into a slice of life

WHAT THE SURGEON TURNED INTO AT THE ANNUAL ROAST.

Now arrange the circled letters to form the surprise answer, as suggested by the above cartoon.

Print answer here A

JUMBLE®

Unscramble these four Jumbles, one letter to each square, to form four ordinary words.

LIPUP

YUNTI

ENGALT

SHEERY

Ed's out like a light

ONE TOO MANY MADE HIM DO THIS.

Now arrange the circled letters to form the surprise answer, as suggested by the above cartoon.

Print answer here

" "

JUMBLE®

Unscramble these four Jumbles, one letter to each square, to form four ordinary words.

GINES

BICAN

THOUPS

DUSARI

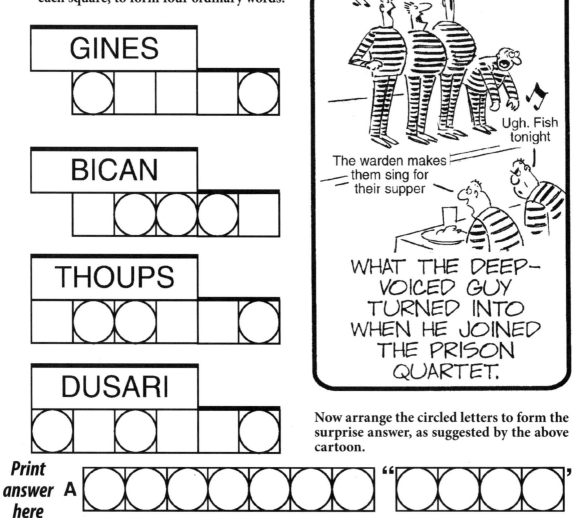

The warden makes them sing for their supper

Ugh. Fish tonight

WHAT THE DEEP-VOICED GUY TURNED INTO WHEN HE JOINED THE PRISON QUARTET.

Now arrange the circled letters to form the surprise answer, as suggested by the above cartoon.

Print answer here A ◯◯◯◯◯◯◯ "◯◯◯◯"

JUMBLE®

Unscramble these four Jumbles, one letter to each square, to form four ordinary words.

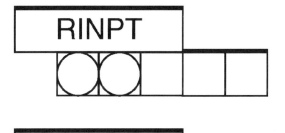

RINPT

FEBOG

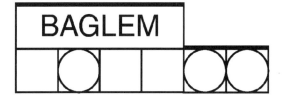

BAGLEM

ENMIRE

I've been up here for three hours. My back is killing me

WHY THE WINDOW WASHER TOOK A BREAK.

Now arrange the circled letters to form the surprise answer, as suggested by the above cartoon.

Print answer here   FOR "  "

JUMBLE®

Unscramble these four Jumbles, one letter to each square, to form four ordinary words.

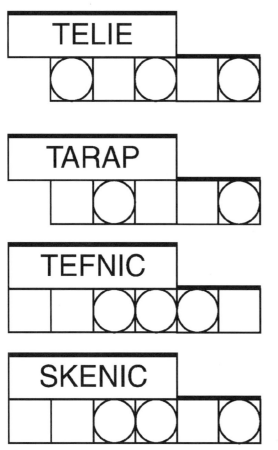

TELIE

TARAP

TEFNIC

SKENIC

Lunch is ready

OFTEN RUNNING AROUND A BACKYARD.

Now arrange the circled letters to form the surprise answer, as suggested by the above cartoon.

Print answer here A

JUMBLE®

Unscramble these four Jumbles, one letter to each square, to form four ordinary words.

NATEC

DYSIA

HASRIG

TENTIK

I'm starving

Me, too

I'll think of something

WHAT MOM FACED WHEN SHE FORGOT TO THAW DINNER.

Now arrange the circled letters to form the surprise answer, as suggested by the above cartoon.

Print answer here "◯◯◯" ◯◯◯◯◯◯

JUMBLE®

Unscramble these four Jumbles, one letter to
each square, to form four ordinary words.

BYGUL

THICY

LEVVET

NULDOA

You should
go home

I'm running
out of
sick days

AACHOO!

WHY THE OPERA-
TOR WENT TO
WORK DESPITE
A HEAVY COLD.

Now arrange the circled letters to form the
surprise answer, as suggested by the above
cartoon.

Print
answer THE "◯◯◯◯" TO ◯◯◯◯
here

JUMBLE®

Unscramble these four Jumbles, one letter to
each square, to form four ordinary words.

SLARN

WROBE

YAXTIL

ICETOX

My wallet
is lighter,
but I'm not

I must have
gained four
pounds

WHAT AN EXPENSIVE
MEAL CAN COST.

Now arrange the circled letters to form the
surprise answer, as suggested by the above
cartoon.

Print
answer
here

A ☐☐☐ OF ☐☐☐☐☐☐☐☐

Unscramble these four Jumbles, one letter to each square, to form four ordinary words.

YUMMG

TAYFF

TOOCLE

TORTOG

A drink in celebration

WHEN HE ORDERED ONE FOR THE ROAD, HE----

Now arrange the circled letters to form the surprise answer, as suggested by the above cartoon.

Print answer here ◯◯◯ A ◯◯◯

JUMBLE®

Unscramble these four Jumbles, one letter to each square, to form four ordinary words.

CUHDY

SUGES

THROME

DABINT

Oh, he's so cute. Can we take him home? Please! Please!

WHAT JUNIOR DID TO DAD AT THE PET SHOP.

Now arrange the circled letters to form the surprise answer, as suggested by the above cartoon.

Print answer here " ⬡⬡⬡⬡⬡⬡⬡ " ⬡⬡⬡

JUMBLE®

Unscramble these four Jumbles, one letter to
each square, to form four ordinary words.

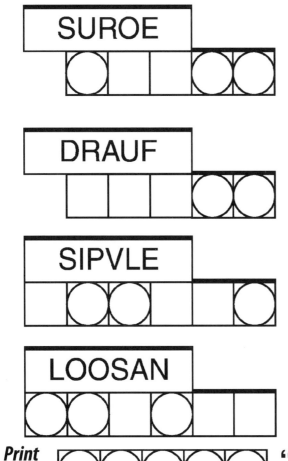

SUROE

DRAUF

SIPVLE

LOOSAN

Too many expenses,
not enough profit

CLOSED

WHY THE SWEET
SHOP WENT OUT
OF BUSINESS.

Now arrange the circled letters to form the
surprise answer, as suggested by the above
cartoon.

*Print
answer
here*

" "

JUMBLE®

Unscramble these four Jumbles, one letter to each square, to form four ordinary words.

VALIE

VAROS

THIBLE

THINGK

Wow! A card, flowers, candy, and dinner

MANY WILL DO THIS ON VALENTINE'S DAY.

Now arrange the circled letters to form the surprise answer, as suggested by the above cartoon.

Print answer here ⬡⬡⬡⬡ IT TO "⬡⬡⬡⬡⬡"

JUMBLE®

Unscramble these four Jumbles, one letter to
each square, to form four ordinary words.

GEDUN

DYNOW

NOPETT

NAYYAW

Help me with
the groceries

This is yummy

WHAT THE CHIL-
DREN DID WHEN
MOM BROUGHT
HOME COOKIES.

Now arrange the circled letters to form the
surprise answer, as suggested by the above
cartoon.

Print
answer
here

" ◯◯◯ " THEM " ◯◯◯◯ "

JUMBLE®

Unscramble these four Jumbles, one letter to each square, to form four ordinary words.

DORRA

THRIM

YOCKEJ

DINCAR

Every time you move, you squeak like a mouse

Who, me?

WHEN THE KNIGHT MADE A SNIDE REMARK, IT RESULTED IN A----

Now arrange the circled letters to form the surprise answer, as suggested by the above cartoon.

Print answer here " ◯◯◯◯◯ " IN HIS ◯◯◯◯◯

JUMBLE

Unscramble these four Jumbles, one letter to
each square, to form four ordinary words.

UNGTS

GEWIH

DROAFE

LEMOTE

Hey — get
back here

WHAT THE SHEP-
HERD DID WHEN
THE MOTHER AND
LAMBS STRAYED
FROM THE FLOCK.

Now arrange the circled letters to form the
surprise answer, as suggested by the above
cartoon.

Print
answer
here

◯◯◯◯◯ A ◯◯◯◯ ◯◯◯◯◯

JUMBLE®

Unscramble these four Jumbles, one letter to each square, to form four ordinary words.

TUMSY

SYNOW

ASCUBA

TUEBAY

It doesn't look like me at all!

HE DESTROYED THE PIECE OF SCULPTURE BECAUSE THE----

Now arrange the circled letters to form the surprise answer, as suggested by the above cartoon.

Print answer here

A

JUMBLE®

Unscramble these four Jumbles, one letter to each square, to form four ordinary words.

STRYT

KRYJE

BERICK

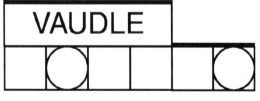

VAUDLE

J.B., what if we offer…

J.B., I suggest we consider…

"AIDES" CAN GIVE YOU THIS.

Now arrange the circled letters to form the surprise answer, as suggested by the above cartoon.

Print answer here

72

JUMBLE®

Unscramble these four Jumbles, one letter to
each square, to form four ordinary words.

MEFAL

KOLEY

LOUGEY

YOHRFT

$50 bonus if you
store all the hay
in one day

Big deal —
that's a
three-day
job

WHAT THE FARMER
GAVE THE HIRED
HANDS.

Now arrange the circled letters to form the
surprise answer, as suggested by the above
cartoon.

*Print
answer   A
here*   "◯◯◯◯◯" ◯◯◯◯

JUMBLE®

Unscramble these four Jumbles, one letter to
each square, to form four ordinary words.

KARCC

WYLLO

KROMES

POURRA

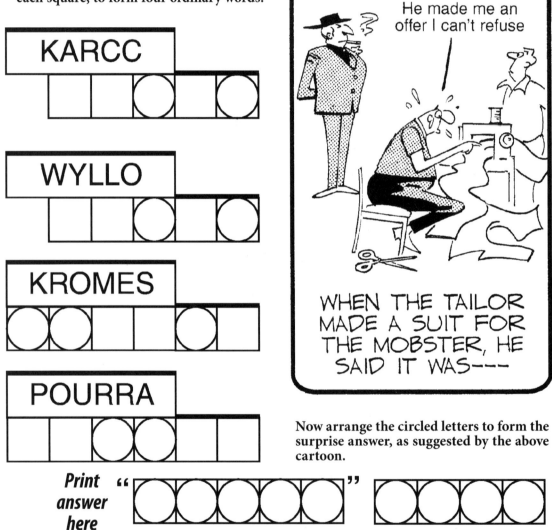

He made me an
offer I can't refuse

WHEN THE TAILOR
MADE A SUIT FOR
THE MOBSTER, HE
SAID IT WAS---

Now arrange the circled letters to form the
surprise answer, as suggested by the above
cartoon.

Print
answer
here

" ⃝⃝⃝⃝⃝ " ⃝⃝⃝⃝

JUMBLE®

Unscramble these four Jumbles, one letter to each square, to form four ordinary words.

TIVER

GAMNY

FLEEBE

WARIAY

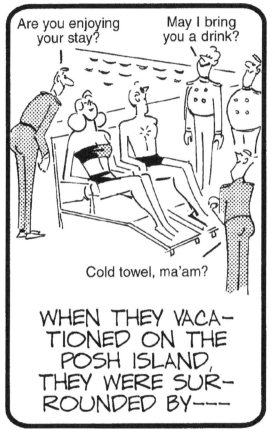

Are you enjoying your stay?

May I bring you a drink?

Cold towel, ma'am?

WHEN THEY VACA-TIONED ON THE POSH ISLAND, THEY WERE SUR-ROUNDED BY---

Now arrange the circled letters to form the surprise answer, as suggested by the above cartoon.

Print answer here

JUMBLE®

Unscramble these four Jumbles, one letter to
each square, to form four ordinary words.

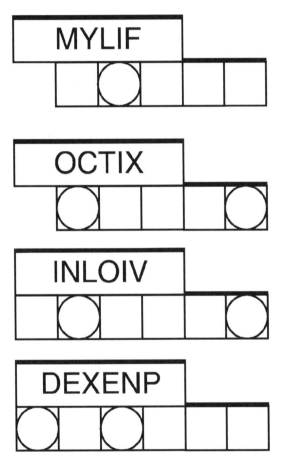

MYLIF

OCTIX

INLOIV

DEXENP

Redwood Boy in
the seventh

WHAT THE BOOKIE
GAVE THE WAITER.

Now arrange the circled letters to form the
surprise answer, as suggested by the above
cartoon.

Print answer here A  "  "

JUMBLE®

Unscramble these four Jumbles, one letter to each square, to form four ordinary words.

YARDT

KLANE

HEETES

CEIVED

STAGE DOOR

Oh, he's gorgeous

I almost touched him

HOW THE STEAMY SOAP OPERA STAR LEFT THE FANS.

Now arrange the circled letters to form the surprise answer, as suggested by the above cartoon.

Print answer here ⬡⬡ A " ⬡⬡⬡⬡⬡⬡ "

JUMBLE®

Unscramble these four Jumbles, one letter to each square, to form four ordinary words.

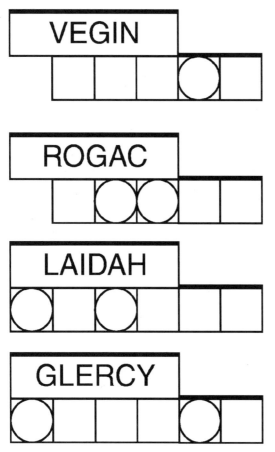

VEGIN

ROGAC

LAIDAH

GLERCY

WHAT THE DETEC-
TIVES DID WHEN
THEY SPOTTED THE
CREDIT-CARD
THIEVES.

Now arrange the circled letters to form the surprise answer, as suggested by the above cartoon.

Print answer here " ◯◯◯◯◯◯◯ "

JUMBLE®

Unscramble these four Jumbles, one letter to each square, to form four ordinary words.

RUSUY

DOTUB

NYWIRT

SITMIF

Harry, you know sausage isn't good for you

It's OK, Myrna. I'll take a pill

WHEN TOURING GERMANY, THE ULCER SUFFERER TOOK A----

Now arrange the circled letters to form the surprise answer, as suggested by the above cartoon.

Print answer here

FOR THE " "

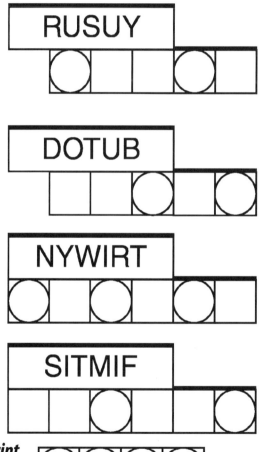

79

JUMBLE®

Unscramble these four Jumbles, one letter to each square, to form four ordinary words.

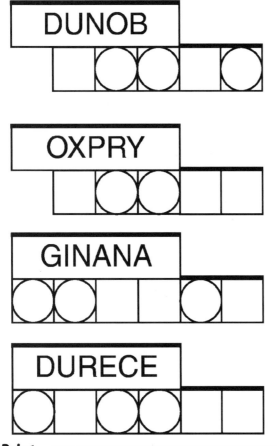

DUNOB

OXPRY

GINANA

DURECE

He lasted less than two minutes

...and still champion

HOW LONG DID THE CHALLENGER LAST AGAINST THE CHAMP?

Now arrange the circled letters to form the surprise answer, as suggested by the above cartoon.

Print answer here

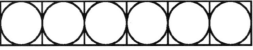 A

JUMBLE®

Unscramble these four Jumbles, one letter to each square, to form four ordinary words.

DAIDE

LIDAP

NAWKEE

THORAU

Craps again. Gimme another (hic) drink

WHAT THE TIPSY GAMBLER AND THE DICE HAD IN COMMON.

Now arrange the circled letters to form the surprise answer, as suggested by the above cartoon.

Print answer here   THEY ⬤⬤⬤⬤ " ⬤⬤⬤⬤⬤⬤⬤ "

JUMBLE.

Unscramble these four Jumbles, one letter to
each square, to form four ordinary words.

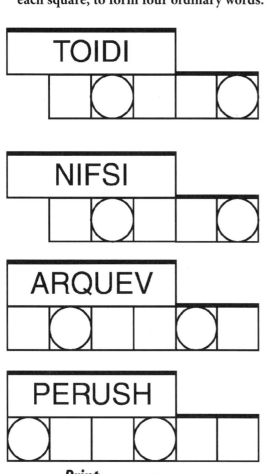

TOIDI

NIFSI

ARQUEV

PERUSH

It's your turn
to wash

No, it's
yours

WHAT THE KIDS
FACED AFTER
DINNER.

Now arrange the circled letters to form the
surprise answer, as suggested by the above
cartoon.

*Print
answer* **A**
here

" ⬡⬡⬡⬡ - ⬡⬡⬡⬡ "

JUMBLE.

Unscramble these four Jumbles, one letter to
each square, to form four ordinary words.

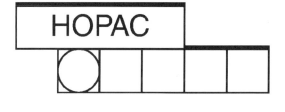

HOPAC

REFAT

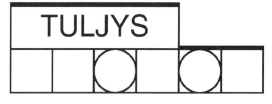

TULJYS

ELLBOW

Good boy. Let's
get back to work

WHAT THE TRAINER
GAVE THE GREY-
HOUND DURING
HIS MORNING
WORKOUT.

Now arrange the circled letters to form the
surprise answer, as suggested by the above
cartoon.

Print answer here A ◯◯◯ " ◯◯◯◯ "

JUMBLE®

Unscramble these four Jumbles, one letter to
each square, to form four ordinary words.

RYSAC

RYBIN

PERUPA

SHARTH

Caught him red-handed

We chased him three flights

WHEN THE ROBBER
WAS CAUGHT ON
THE STEPS,
THE COPS SAID
IT WAS——

Now arrange the circled letters to form the
surprise answer, as suggested by the above
cartoon.

Print
answer A
here

"   "

JUMBLE®

Unscramble these four Jumbles, one letter to each square, to form four ordinary words.

THYAS

LEBIE

GRONTS

EURUFT

Tell them to go back to sleep

LESS TAX

MORE PAY

=

WHAT THE KING EXPERIENCED WHEN HE WAS AWAKENED BY THE PROTESTERS.

Now arrange the circled letters to form the surprise answer, as suggested by the above cartoon.

Print answer here

A ☐OOOOO OF "OOOOOO"

JUMBLE®

Unscramble these four Jumbles, one letter to
each square, to form four ordinary words.

LAQUI

JEGUD

PITTEE

THACLE

I'm taking Rex
for a walk

KNOWN TO LEAVE
WHEN TEENAGERS
HAVE THEIR
FRIENDS OVER.

Now arrange the circled letters to form the
surprise answer, as suggested by the above
cartoon.

**Print
answer
here** ⬡⬡⬡⬡⬡ **AND** ⬡⬡⬡⬡⬡

JUMBLE®

Unscramble these four Jumbles, one letter to
each square, to form four ordinary words.

VAREN

VOYEC

GLUTLE

RAYLEY

We need every able body
to help prevent a flood

And lots of
tax dollars

WHAT IT TOOK
TO SANDBAG THE
TOWN AGAINST THE
RISING RIVER.

Now arrange the circled letters to form the
surprise answer, as suggested by the above
cartoon.

*Print
answer* A
here

JUMBLE®

Unscramble these four Jumbles, one letter to each square, to form four ordinary words.

LAGIE

PLIMB

NEMDIP

DIMPIL

Two minutes for rebuttal, sir

HE DIDN'T TAKE SIDES IN THE DEBATE BECAUSE HE WAS A----

Now arrange the circled letters to form the surprise answer, as suggested by the above cartoon.

Print answer here " ⟨ ⟩⟨ ⟩⟨ ⟩⟨ ⟩⟨ ⟩⟨ ⟩ " ⟨ ⟩⟨ ⟩⟨ ⟩

JUMBLE®

Unscramble these four Jumbles, one letter to each square, to form four ordinary words.

TOINX

YORFE

DORMIB

HUNGOE

Let's take (yawn) 20 minutes for a recess

WHEN THE JUDGE PRESIDED OVER THE LONG TRIAL, HE---

Now arrange the circled letters to form the surprise answer, as suggested by the above cartoon.

Print answer here

⬡⬡⬡⬡⬡ IT " ⬡⬡⬡⬡⬡⬡ "

JUMBLE®

Unscramble these four Jumbles, one letter to each square, to form four ordinary words.

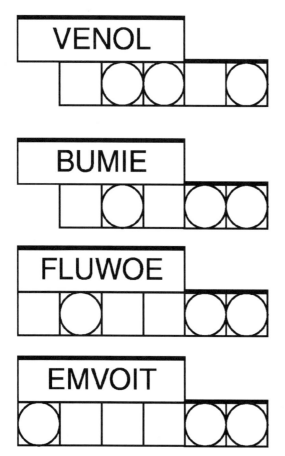

VENOL

BUMIE

FLUWOE

EMVOIT

And then they embraced

Turn it up a little

Use the headset

WHAT THEY NEEDED TO LISTEN TO THE BOOK ON TAPE.

Now arrange the circled letters to form the surprise answer, as suggested by the above cartoon.

Print answer here

JUMBLE.

Unscramble these four Jumbles, one letter to each square, to form four ordinary words.

KOBOR

NOOLC

CARBIF

SUTTOM

They're all leaving

GO HOME === BOO

WHERE THE BAND ENDED UP WHEN THEIR CONCERT FIZZLED.

Now arrange the circled letters to form the surprise answer, as suggested by the above cartoon.

Print answer here AT " ◯◯◯◯ " ◯◯◯◯◯◯◯

JUMBLE®

Unscramble these four Jumbles, one letter to each square, to form four ordinary words.

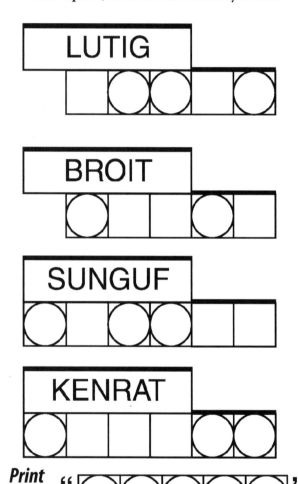

LUTIG

BROIT

SUNGUF

KENRAT

Stay under the umbrella, your majesty

WHEN THE KING WENT OUT FOR THE NIGHT, HE WORE HIS----

Now arrange the circled letters to form the surprise answer, as suggested by the above cartoon.

Print answer here " ⃝⃝⃝⃝⃝ " ⃝⃝⃝⃝⃝⃝

JUMBLE®

Unscramble these four Jumbles, one letter to each square, to form four ordinary words.

EGGRO

CUFOS

TENCED

GARNAL

They'll never look for us here

Nothing but lovely blue skies today. High 85°

WHY THE ROBBERS HEADED FOR THE SEASHORE.

Now arrange the circled letters to form the surprise answer, as suggested by the above cartoon.

Print answer here THE ◯◯◯◯◯ WAS " ◯◯◯◯◯ "

JUMBLE®

Unscramble these four Jumbles, one letter to
each square, to form four ordinary words.

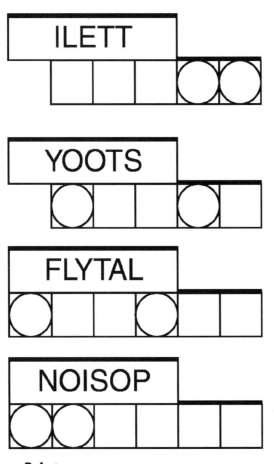

ILETT

YOOTS

FLYTAL

NOISOP

Any letters
for me?

I forgot to
bring them

THE JOCKEY'S MAIL
DIDN'T ARRIVE
BECAUSE IT WAS----

Now arrange the circled letters to form the
surprise answer, as suggested by the above
cartoon.

*Print
answer
here*
 AT THE "  "

JUMBLE®

Unscramble these four Jumbles, one letter to each square, to form four ordinary words.

TOBAB

DETES

ROHORR

ROZNEF

Sleep it off

I don't feel so good

HOW THE DRUNKEN COWBOY FELT WHEN THE SHERIFF PUT HIM IN THE COOLER.

Now arrange the circled letters to form the surprise answer, as suggested by the above cartoon.

Print answer here

JUMBLE®

Unscramble these four Jumbles, one letter to each square, to form four ordinary words.

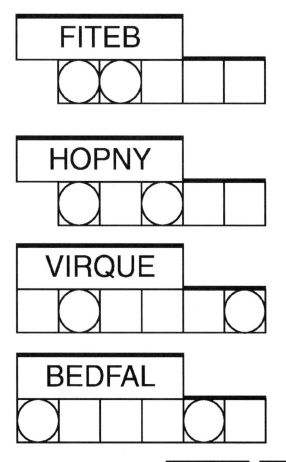

FITEB

HOPNY

VIRQUE

BEDFAL

I had to set the alarm for 5:00 AM

WHEN THE JUDGE HAD AN EARLY COURT CALL, HE FOUND DEFENDANTS----

Now arrange the circled letters to form the surprise answer, as suggested by the above cartoon.

Print answer here ◯◯ ◯◯◯◯◯◯◯ HIM

JUMBLE®

Unscramble these four Jumbles, one letter to each square, to form four ordinary words.

LEROD

WAKTE

HASFIM

FORFET

C'mon, buy a broom. Why are you so cheap?

Go away

WHY THE DOOR-TO-DOOR SALES-MAN WAS SPURNED.

Now arrange the circled letters to form the surprise answer, as suggested by the above cartoon.

Print answer here HE " ☐☐☐☐☐ " ☐☐☐ ☐☐

JUMBLE®

Unscramble these four Jumbles, one letter to each square, to form four ordinary words.

GOUCH

CHATY

PINKAD

STEWEN

$5,000? It's my birthday
OUCH!! present

WHEN SHE GOT
THE BILL FOR
THE DIAMOND
PIN, HE GOT----

Now arrange the circled letters to form the surprise answer, as suggested by the above cartoon.

Print answer here " ◯◯◯◯◯ " ◯◯◯◯ IT

JUMBLE®

Unscramble these four Jumbles, one letter to each square, to form four ordinary words.

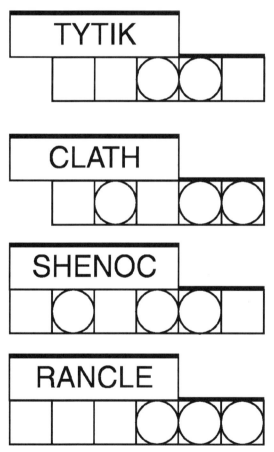

TYTIK

CLATH

SHENOC

RANCLE

This isn't working

Pull down the bar

WHAT HE DISCOV-ERED WHEN HE TRIED TO OPEN THE LATCH.

Now arrange the circled letters to form the surprise answer, as suggested by the above cartoon.

Print answer here

' A

JUMBLE®

Unscramble these four Jumbles, one letter to each square, to form four ordinary words.

DRAIP

DUNTE

BIMTAG

CUNESS

Right down the middle

Oops. I forgot my clubs

THE PROFESSOR SKIPPED CLASS ON A BALMY DAY BECAUSE HE WAS----

Now arrange the circled letters to form the surprise answer, as suggested by the above cartoon.

Print answer here " ◯◯◯◯◯ " ◯◯◯◯◯◯

JUMBLE®

Unscramble these four Jumbles, one letter to each square, to form four ordinary words.

DELOY

ALOCK

RANOUD

LEZZUP

I don't even have time for lunch

HOW THE LOCK-SMITH FELT ON A BUSY DAY.

Now arrange the circled letters to form the surprise answer, as suggested by the above cartoon.

Print answer here

" "

JUMBLE®

Unscramble these four Jumbles, one letter to each square, to form four ordinary words.

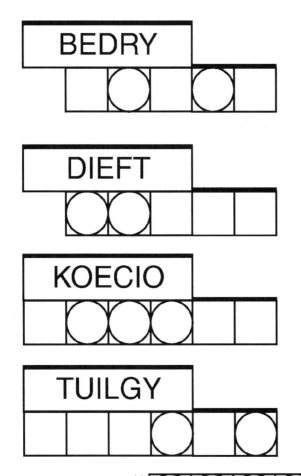

BEDRY

DIEFT

KOECIO

TUILGY

That steak sure smells good

ALTHOUGH HE WAS A VEGETARIAN, THE DINER HAD A----

Now arrange the circled letters to form the surprise answer, as suggested by the above cartoon.

Print answer here " ◯◯◯◯◯ " ◯◯◯◯

JUMBLE®

Unscramble these four Jumbles, one letter to each square, to form four ordinary words.

ENSIO

CAFTE

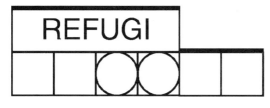

HALNIE

REFUGI

Nice job, Miss Jones

WHEN THE BOSS GAVE HER A PAT ON THE SHOULDER, SHE FOUND IT----

Now arrange the circled letters to form the surprise answer, as suggested by the above cartoon.

Print answer here " ◯◯◯◯◯◯◯◯ "

JUMBLE®

Unscramble these four Jumbles, one letter to
each square, to form four ordinary words.

KWONN

NAUHM

SOYSIF

SEIBED

I'll take the bracelet
and the fur

WHAT SHE GOT
WHEN HE TOOK
HER SHOPPING.

Now arrange the circled letters to form the
surprise answer, as suggested by the above
cartoon.

Print answer here

JUMBLE®

Unscramble these four Jumbles, one letter to
each square, to form four ordinary words.

TELOX

MORRA

VISNAH

BROTED

Cut it short, like
it used to be

WHEN HER HAIR
RETURNED TO ITS
NATURAL COLOR,
SHE WENT BACK
TO---

Now arrange the circled letters to form the
surprise answer, as suggested by the above
cartoon.

Print answer here

JUMBLE®

Unscramble these four Jumbles, one letter to
each square, to form four ordinary words.

LIVIG

GLIYN

CRESPO

RAWHTT

He makes
a big
difference

WHAT A SEVEN-FOOT
CENTER CAN BE
TO A BASKETBALL
TEAM.

Now arrange the circled letters to form the
surprise answer, as suggested by the above
cartoon.

Print answer here " ◯◯◯◯◯ - ◯◯ "

106

JUMBLE®

Unscramble these four Jumbles, one letter to each square, to form four ordinary words.

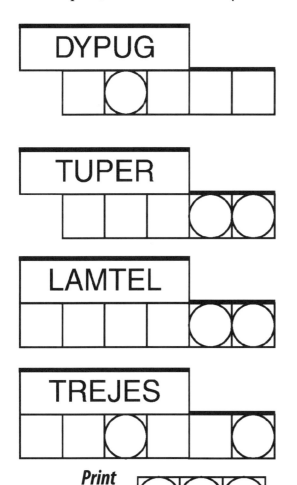

DYPUG

TUPER

LAMTEL

TREJES

Fine. Let's get the queen size

Fine with me

WHEN THEY SETTLED THEIR DISAGREEMENT OVER A NEW BED, THEY----

Now arrange the circled letters to form the surprise answer, as suggested by the above cartoon.

Print answer here ⬡⬡⬡ IT TO " ⬡⬡⬡⬡ "

JUMBLE®

Unscramble these four Jumbles, one letter to each square, to form four ordinary words.

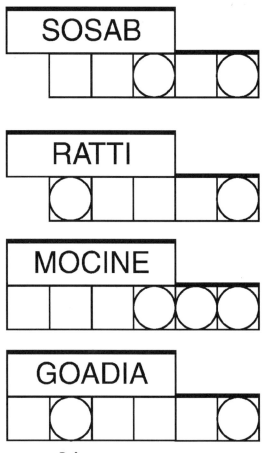

SOSAB

RATTI

MOCINE

GOADIA

That's all
I get?

I took
out taxes
and insurance

THE EXOTIC DANCER
QUIT BECAUSE HER
PAYCHECK WAS----

Now arrange the circled letters to form the surprise answer, as suggested by the above cartoon.

Print answer here

" "

JUMBLE®

Unscramble these four Jumbles, one letter to each square, to form four ordinary words.

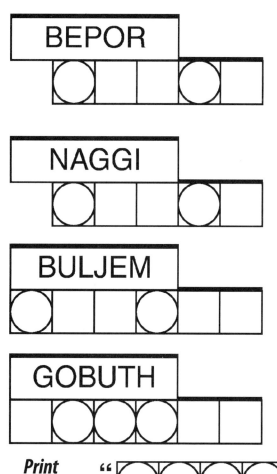

BEPOR

NAGGI

BULJEM

GOBUTH

They put on a good show

Wow! That's some crash

WHAT THE DRIVERS DID IN THE DEMO-LITION DERBY.

Now arrange the circled letters to form the surprise answer, as suggested by the above cartoon.

Print answer here A "◯◯◯◯-◯◯" ◯◯◯

JUMBLE®

Unscramble these four Jumbles, one letter to
each square, to form four ordinary words.

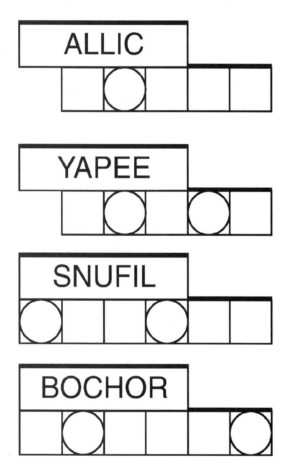

ALLIC

YAPEE

SNUFIL

BOCHOR

She's very objective

...And easy to
look at

WHY THE BLOND
NEWSCASTER
MODERATED
THE DEBATE.

Now arrange the circled letters to form the
surprise answer, as suggested by the above
cartoon.

Print answer here ◯◯◯ WAS " ◯◯◯◯ "

JUMBLE®

Unscramble these four Jumbles, one letter to each square, to form four ordinary words.

HIEWL

YEDIT

NOVISI

BAHFLE

But, Ms. Thistlewood, this area was supposed to be a lounge

We needed room for more books

WHAT THE LIBRARIAN DID TO THE REMODELING PLAN.

Now arrange the circled letters to form the surprise answer, as suggested by the above cartoon.

Print answer here " ⬡⬡⬡⬡⬡⬡⬡ " IT

JUMBLE®

Unscramble these four Jumbles, one letter to
each square, to form four ordinary words.

GUBOH

AZERC

CUSSID

PAWNEO

Charlie, stop
by my office

MGR

AFTER HITTING
THE SHOWERS,
THE AGING
PITCHER WAS---

Now arrange the circled letters to form the
surprise answer, as suggested by the above
cartoon.

Print answer here " ◯◯◯◯◯◯ " ◯◯

JUMBLE®

Unscramble these four Jumbles, one letter to each square, to form four ordinary words.

SULPH

SUGIE

VAHBEE

BLYMAC

Welcome back, sir. You look great

It was expensive, but I lost 30 pounds

WHAT HE ENDED UP WITH WHEN HE PAID GOOD MONEY TO LOSE WEIGHT.

Now arrange the circled letters to form the surprise answer, as suggested by the above cartoon.

Print answer here ⬡⬡⬡⬡ OF ⬡⬡⬡⬡

JUMBLE®

Unscramble these four Jumbles, one letter to each square, to form four ordinary words.

COEMA

PHESE

REBAYT

DYRAHL

NOW PLAYING

It's not as good as the book

WHEN THE BEST-SELLING BIOGRAPHY BECAME A MOVIE, IT TURNED INTO---

Now arrange the circled letters to form the surprise answer, as suggested by the above cartoon.

Print answer here   THE "⬡⬡⬡⬡" ⬡⬡⬡⬡⬡

JUMBLE®

Unscramble these four Jumbles, one letter to each square, to form four ordinary words.

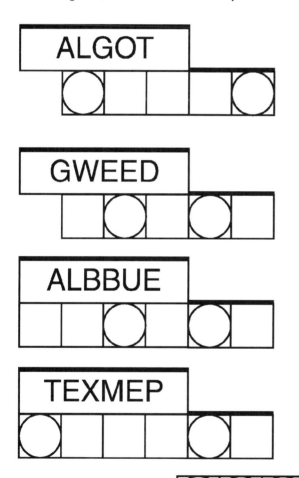

ALGOT

GWEED

ALBBUE

TEXMEP

He'll increase sales

Our competitors won't be happy

THE RUNNING-SHOE COMPANY HIRED THE SPRINTER TO ----

Now arrange the circled letters to form the surprise answer, as suggested by the above cartoon.

Print answer here  A

JUMBLE®

Unscramble these four Jumbles, one letter to
each square, to form four ordinary words.

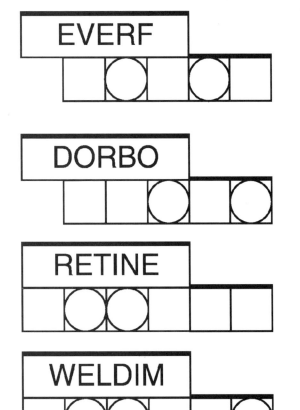

EVERF

DORBO

RETINE

WELDIM

I just stopped for a minute

You broke the law

NO PARKING

WHEN THE
ILLEGALLY PARKED
CARS BLOCKED
TRAFFIC, THE
COP---

Now arrange the circled letters to form the
surprise answer, as suggested by the above
cartoon.

Print answer here ⬡⬡⬡⬡⬡ THE ⬡⬡⬡⬡

JUMBLE®

Unscramble these four Jumbles, one letter to each square, to form four ordinary words.

NEWIT

WOYDD

MURQUO

YURKET

That's not appropriate

But I'm comfortable

WHY HE COULDN'T GO TO THE DINNER PARTY IN HIS FAVORITE SHIRT.

Now arrange the circled letters to form the surprise answer, as suggested by the above cartoon.

Print answer here IT WAS " ⬡⬡⬡⬡ " ⬡⬡⬡

JUMBLE®

Unscramble these four Jumbles, one letter to
each square, to form four ordinary words.

DRUIL

MORIN

GAMANE

SATECK

That's very
touching

I'm very
sentimental

WHEN THE GANG-
STER GOT A
TATTOO, HE
BECAME A----

Now arrange the circled letters to form the
surprise answer, as suggested by the above
cartoon.

*Print
answer
here* "◯◯◯◯◯◯◯" ◯◯◯

JUMBLE®

Unscramble these four Jumbles, one letter to each square, to form four ordinary words.

DANSY

YORRS

REEVER

YOBUDE

I'd like some geraniums and pansies

WHERE MOM TOOK HER TODDLER WHEN SHE WENT SHOPPING.

Now arrange the circled letters to form the surprise answer, as suggested by the above cartoon.

Print answer here TO THE " ⬡⬡⬡⬡⬡⬡⬡ "

JUMBLE®

Unscramble these four Jumbles, one letter to
each square, to form four ordinary words.

TIHHC

KALCH

SIXECE

EXDOUT

You owe an
additional
$1,000 dollars

A pox on
your house

IRS

WHAT THE ANGRY
WITCH GAVE THE
TAX COLLECTOR.

Now arrange the circled letters to form the
surprise answer, as suggested by the above
cartoon.

Print answer here A " ◯◯◯ " ◯◯◯◯

120

JUMBLE®

Unscramble these four Jumbles, one letter to each square, to form four ordinary words.

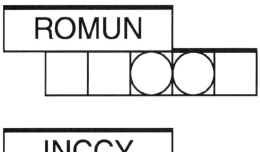

ROMUN

INCCY

YEARTT

DRENER

Boy, that looks heavy

Wonderful player, but he can't sing

WHAT THE BASS FIDDLER FOUND TOUGH TO DO.

Now arrange the circled letters to form the surprise answer, as suggested by the above cartoon.

Print answer here

◯◯◯◯◯ A ◯◯◯◯

JUMBLE®

Unscramble these four Jumbles, one letter to each square, to form four ordinary words.

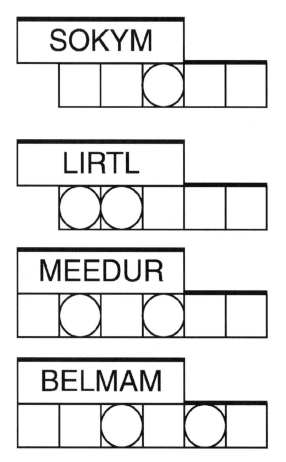

SOKYM

LIRTL

MEEDUR

BELMAM

No raise—no work!

Oh, really?

THIS WAS BREWING AT THE BEER MAKER.

Now arrange the circled letters to form the surprise answer, as suggested by the above cartoon.

Print answer here " ◯◯◯◯◯◯◯◯ "

JUMBLE®

Unscramble these four Jumbles, one letter to
each square, to form four ordinary words.

LUFAW

GACIM

NOOTIL

RAZABA

We'll have
to let
the sleeves
down

WHEN THE POLICE-
MAN BOUGHT A
NEW UNIFORM, THE
TAILOR ALTERED
THE---

Now arrange the circled letters to form the
surprise answer, as suggested by the above
cartoon.

**Print
answer
here** ◯◯◯◯ ◯◯◯ OF THE ◯◯◯

JUMBLE®

Unscramble these four Jumbles, one letter to
each square, to form four ordinary words.

HINEW

TOFLY

VAINED

WAHLIE

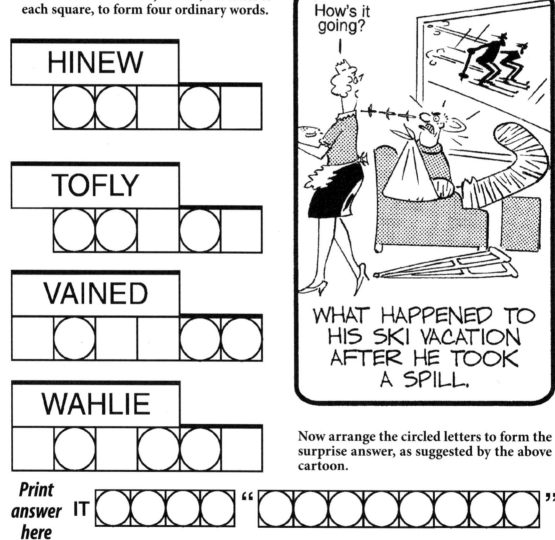

How's it going?

WHAT HAPPENED TO
HIS SKI VACATION
AFTER HE TOOK
A SPILL.

Now arrange the circled letters to form the
surprise answer, as suggested by the above
cartoon.

**Print
answer
here** IT ◯◯◯◯ " ◯◯◯◯◯◯◯◯◯ "

JUMBLE®

Unscramble these four Jumbles, one letter to each square, to form four ordinary words.

KAROC

CEPEN

EEDDAC

ENNKLE

I'll be right—

OUCH!

WHEN THE WINDOW CAME DOWN ON HIM, HE SAID IT WAS A---

Now arrange the circled letters to form the surprise answer, as suggested by the above cartoon.

Print answer here " ⬭⬭⬭⬭ " IN THE ⬭⬭⬭⬭

Unscramble these four Jumbles, one letter to
each square, to form four ordinary words.

BECAL

RYMEC

THUNGA

TABEED

Going 50. Pull over
to the side

What did
I do?

30
MPH

WHAT CITY COPS
SEEK TO DO
WITH SPEEDING
MOTORISTS.

Now arrange the circled letters to form the
surprise answer, as suggested by the above
cartoon.

Print answer here "⃝⃝⃝⃝" ⃝⃝⃝⃝

JUMBLE®

Unscramble these four Jumbles, one letter to
each square, to form four ordinary words.

ENCEF

LIMYK

PHOCON

BIMBIE

She'll be in the
kitchen for days

WHERE SHE ENDED
UP WHEN THE
CUCUMBER CROP
WAS HARVESTED.

Now arrange the circled letters to form the
surprise answer, as suggested by the above
cartoon.

Print answer here ⬚⬚ A " ⬚⬚⬚⬚⬚⬚ "

JUMBLE®

Unscramble these four Jumbles, one letter to each square, to form four ordinary words.

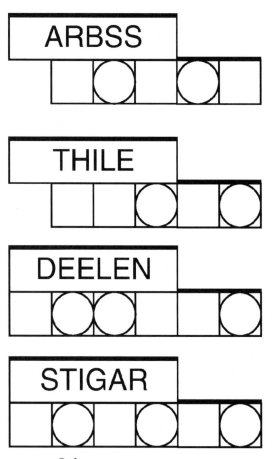

ARBSS

THILE

DEELEN

STIGAR

Git them dogies back here, Tex

WHAT COWBOYS DO ON THE RANGE.

Now arrange the circled letters to form the surprise answer, as suggested by the above cartoon.

Print answer here

JUMBLE®

Unscramble these four Jumbles, one letter to each square, to form four ordinary words.

KORJE

NITLE

BANDOU

DOLITS

I've got a headache and can't focus

SPENDING HOURS LOOKING THROUGH A TELE-SCOPE GAVE THE ASTRONOMER A---

Now arrange the circled letters to form the surprise answer, as suggested by the above cartoon.

Print answer here " ⬡⬡⬡⬡⬡⬡⬡ " ⬡⬡⬡⬡

JUMBLE®

Unscramble these four Jumbles, one letter to each square, to form four ordinary words.

FLUTA

DROAH

SELING

RUMABI

That's longer than the aisle

WHY THE BRIDE DIDN'T WANT A TRAIN ON HER WEDDING GOWN.

Now arrange the circled letters to form the surprise answer, as suggested by the above cartoon.

Print answer here ◯◯ ' ◯ A " ◯◯◯◯ "

JUMBLE®

Unscramble these four Jumbles, one letter to
each square, to form four ordinary words.

RATYR

HUTOY

WASALY

AWBEER

It's been in the
family for four
generations

SHE KEPT THE
HAND-ME-DOWN
CHEST BECAUSE
IT WAS---

Now arrange the circled letters to form the
surprise answer, as suggested by the above
cartoon.

Print answer here A " "

131

JUMBLE®

Unscramble these four Jumbles, one letter to each square, to form four ordinary words.

BALEF

NOONI

VACTAR

TOCIPE

We have VIP passes

Right this way

WHAT THEY USED TO JOIN THE IN-CROWD AT THE HOT DANCE CLUB.

Now arrange the circled letters to form the surprise answer, as suggested by the above cartoon.

Print answer here THE ⬡⬡⬡⬡⬡⬡⬡⬡

JUMBLE®

Unscramble these four Jumbles, one letter to each square, to form four ordinary words.

PIGER

BLAWR

TRAIPY

PYSEDE

The machine won't take it

Caught you red-handed

THE THIEF WAS ARRESTED BECAUSE THE CREDIT CARD WAS---

Now arrange the circled letters to form the surprise answer, as suggested by the above cartoon.

Print answer here " ◯◯◯◯◯◯ "

JUMBLE

Unscramble these four Jumbles, one letter to
each square, to form four ordinary words.

EIDUG

URRJO

LARREB

YALTER

Pick me up at four
with the carriage

Yes,
m'dear

WHAT THE HEN-
PECKED KING
CONSIDERED
HIS WIFE.

Now arrange the circled letters to form the
surprise answer, as suggested by the above
cartoon.

Print
answer THE
here

JUMBLE.

Unscramble these four Jumbles, one letter to each square, to form four ordinary words.

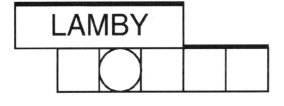

LAMBY

SURNP

SPYNAP

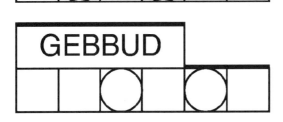

GEBBUD

He started out as a teller

Congratulations, J.D.

He's very trustworthy

THE BANK MANAGER ROSE TO THE TOP BECAUSE HE WAS----

Now arrange the circled letters to form the surprise answer, as suggested by the above cartoon.

Print answer here ON THE

JUMBLE®

Unscramble these four Jumbles, one letter to each square, to form four ordinary words.

YACKT

SKUYD

DORWAT

YATCCH

How do you like your new look?

They're right. I'm not finding as much fun

WHAT THE BLONDE EXPERIENCED WHEN SHE BECAME A BRUNETTE.

Now arrange the circled letters to form the surprise answer, as suggested by the above cartoon.

Print answer here   HER " ◯◯◯◯ " ◯◯◯◯

JUMBLE®

Unscramble these four Jumbles, one letter to
each square, to form four ordinary words.

ALLIV

NELIR

CEMESH

TOARRO

You look sick

I think I've got a fever

HOW THE SOLDIER
FELT AT ROLL
CALL.

Now arrange the circled letters to form the
surprise answer, as suggested by the above
cartoon.

Print answer here

JUMBLE®

Unscramble these four Jumbles, one letter to each square, to form four ordinary words.

DIPEW

SEERA

COMIAT

CHORCS

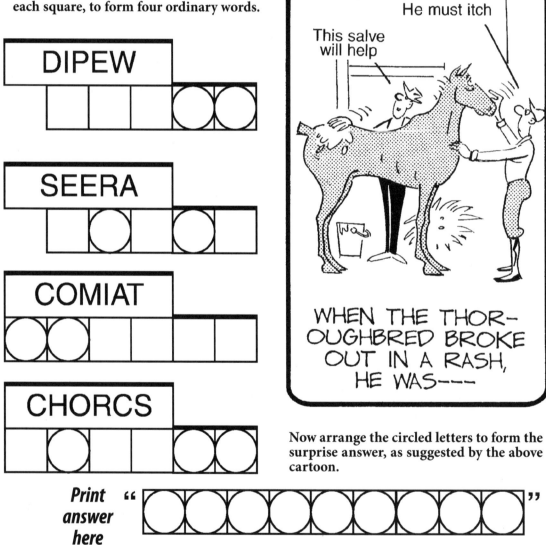

He must itch

This salve will help

WHEN THE THOR-
OUGHBRED BROKE
OUT IN A RASH,
HE WAS----

Now arrange the circled letters to form the surprise answer, as suggested by the above cartoon.

Print answer here " _____ "

JUMBLE®

Unscramble these four Jumbles, one letter to each square, to form four ordinary words.

SAGYS

TEMPY

PRONED

GELISH

I'll drive tomorrow. Same time

DAILY BUGLE

WHAT THE EDITOR AND THE TAILOR SHARED IN THEIR DAILY ROUTINE.

Now arrange the circled letters to form the surprise answer, as suggested by the above cartoon.

Print answer here

" "
TO

JUMBLE®

Unscramble these four Jumbles, one letter to each square, to form four ordinary words.

STYTE

HABET

REPUMB

TORREC

They'll never guess my identity

WHEN THE SPY WORE A WIG, IT WAS----

Now arrange the circled letters to form the surprise answer, as suggested by the above cartoon.

Print answer here " ⟨ ⟩⟨ ⟩⟨ ⟩ " ⟨ ⟩⟨ ⟩⟨ ⟩⟨ ⟩⟨ ⟩⟨ ⟩⟨ ⟩

JUMBLE®

Unscramble these four Jumbles, one letter to each square, to form four ordinary words.

YEASS

OLHLE

THRENE

SHILER

That's why he gets the big money

It's a dangerous job

WHAT THE ANIMAL TRAINER WAS PAID FOR HIS CIRCUS ACT.

Now arrange the circled letters to form the surprise answer, as suggested by the above cartoon.

Print answer here

THE ⬜⬜⬜⬜ ' ⬜ ⬜⬜⬜⬜⬜⬜

JUMBLE®

Unscramble these four Jumbles, one letter to
each square, to form four ordinary words.

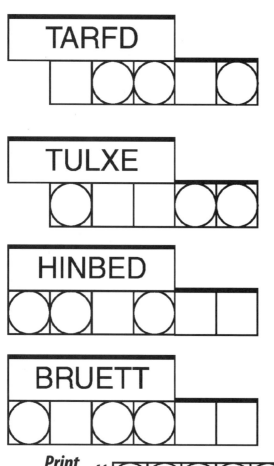

TARFD

TULXE

HINBED

BRUETT

WE WON'T BE UNDER-SOLD

NEITHER WILL WE

WHEN THE RIVAL
"SWEET" SHOPS HAD
A PRICE WAR, THEY
ENDED UP IN A----

Now arrange the circled letters to form the
surprise answer, as suggested by the above
cartoon.

Print
answer
here

"◯◯◯◯◯" ◯◯◯◯◯◯

JUMBLE®

Unscramble these four Jumbles, one letter to
each square, to form four ordinary words.

NAPOC

JECET

INSHIF

FEINED

Hail, hail the
gang's...

He sings
like he
threw
today

SENT TO THE
SHOWERS, THE
HURLER
REMAINED----

Now arrange the circled letters to form the
surprise answer, as suggested by the above
cartoon.

Print answer here 　"　"

JUMBLE®

Unscramble these four Jumbles, one letter to each square, to form four ordinary words.

VAINE

YANER

SOUNIC

GOTSDY

I'm always inspired when I see this

WHEN REVEILLE WAS SOUNDED, THE COMMANDER SAID IT WAS A----

Now arrange the circled letters to form the surprise answer, as suggested by the above cartoon.

Print answer here " ◯◯◯◯◯◯◯ " ◯◯◯◯◯

JUMBLE®

Unscramble these four Jumbles, one letter to each square, to form four ordinary words.

RAWFE

LARNG

NAMMDA

WEEYAL

Will you make me a scarf with this yarn?

WHAT HIS BUDDIES GAVE HIM WHEN HE TOOK UP KNITTING.

Now arrange the circled letters to form the surprise answer, as suggested by the above cartoon.

Print answer here THE " ⬡⬡⬡⬡⬡⬡ "

JUMBLE®

Unscramble these four Jumbles, one letter to each square, to form four ordinary words.

LONBE

DEVEL

SEPPOO

BLOORE

Let's take a look around

WHEN THE SUBMA-RINE REACHED PERISCOPE DEPTH, IT WAS----

Now arrange the circled letters to form the surprise answer, as suggested by the above cartoon.

Print answer **AT** *here*

" ◯◯◯ " ◯◯◯◯◯

146

JUMBLE®

Unscramble these four Jumbles, one letter to each square, to form four ordinary words.

MYDAL

HISFY

ERVEWS

HALMYN

I need this Friday

Me, too

But that's tomorrow

HOW THE SEAM-STRESS FELT BEFORE THE BIG DANCE.

Now arrange the circled letters to form the surprise answer, as suggested by the above cartoon.

Print answer here " ☐☐☐☐☐☐ " ☐☐

JUMBLE®

Unscramble these four Jumbles, one letter to
each square, to form four ordinary words.

GOEBT

WOGIN

KRODEF

KERROB

I'm cramming
all weekend

I've got to
learn 100
pages

WHY THE STUDENT
ROCK BAND DIDN'T
PLAY AT THE PARTY
BEFORE FINALS.

Now arrange the circled letters to form the
surprise answer, as suggested by the above
cartoon.

Print
answer
here   THEY ⬡⬡⬡⬡ " ⬡⬡⬡⬡⬡⬡ "

148

JUMBLE®

Unscramble these four Jumbles, one letter to each square, to form four ordinary words.

THRAW

EEDUL

ROPOLY

BAACAN

asked for medium

Take it or leave it, sir

WHAT THE CUS-TOMER GOT WHEN HIS STEAK WAS UNDERCOOKED.

Now arrange the circled letters to form the surprise answer, as suggested by the above cartoon.

Print answer here A " ⃝⃝⃝ " ⃝⃝⃝⃝

JUMBLE®

Unscramble these four Jumbles, one letter to each square, to form four ordinary words.

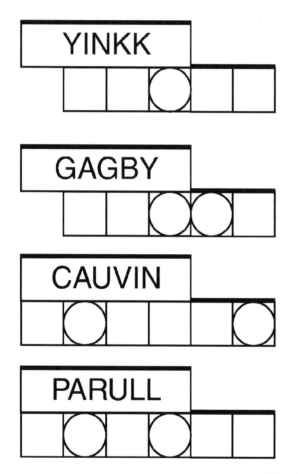

YINKK

GAGBY

CAUVIN

PARULL

How many times have I told them...

ALL THE LIGHTS ON IN THE HOUSE LEFT DAD---

Now arrange the circled letters to form the surprise answer, as suggested by the above cartoon.

Print answer here " ⟨◯◯◯◯◯◯◯⟩ "

JUMBLE.

Unscramble these four Jumbles, one letter to
each square, to form four ordinary words.

THOLC

VINEL

MOAWED

BLARGE

Is my makeup OK?

WHEN THE BOWLER
WAS FILMED FOR
THE AD, HE BECAME
A----

Now arrange the circled letters to form the
surprise answer, as suggested by the above
cartoon.

Print
answer
here " ◯◯◯◯ " ◯◯◯◯◯

JUMBLE®

Unscramble these four Jumbles, one letter to each square, to form four ordinary words.

YOHEN

FITAH

HOKERS

SWETID

One more coat and it's done. It'll dry overnight

WHAT THE FURNI-TURE MAKER WANTED TO DO BEFORE HE WENT HOME.

Now arrange the circled letters to form the surprise answer, as suggested by the above cartoon.

Print answer here " ◯◯◯◯◯◯ " HIS ◯◯◯◯

JUMBLE®

Unscramble these four Jumbles, one letter to each square, to form four ordinary words.

ORDEN

ORVAB

CORHUG

ENCLIP

WHAT THE INVESTI-GATOR DECIDED TO DO AFTER WORKING ALL DAY.

Now arrange the circled letters to form the surprise answer, as suggested by the above cartoon.

Print answer here

JUMBLE®

Unscramble these four Jumbles, one letter to
each square, to form four ordinary words.

BROIN

TOOBA

WYSORD

WABUSY

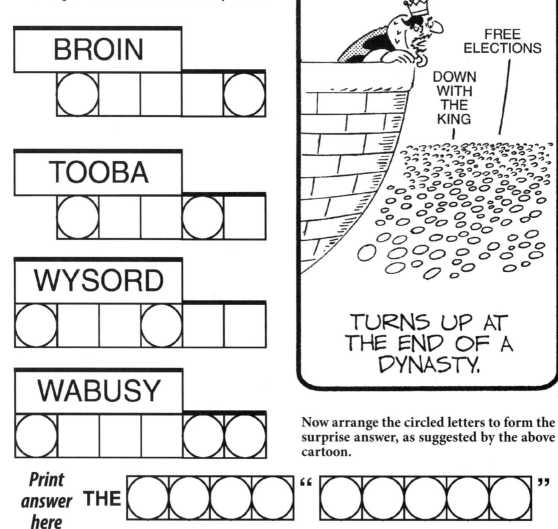

FREE
ELECTIONS

DOWN
WITH
THE
KING

TURNS UP AT
THE END OF A
DYNASTY.

Now arrange the circled letters to form the
surprise answer, as suggested by the above
cartoon.

Print
answer
here
THE ⭕⭕⭕⭕ " ⭕⭕⭕⭕⭕ "

JUMBLE®

Unscramble these four Jumbles, one letter to each square, to form four ordinary words.

GHUDO

GRITE

TASHAG

DHELVA

He'd be mad if I said no

THE FARMER LET HIS SON KEEP THE PET KID BECAUSE HE DIDN'T WANT TO---

Now arrange the circled letters to form the surprise answer, as suggested by the above cartoon.

Print answer here

155

JUMBLE®

Unscramble these four Jumbles, one letter to
each square, to form four ordinary words.

EWTTE

DISAT

FIGNAC

TOINNE

Two hours late.
Oh, well!
Maybe she's not
coming

WHEN HE WAS
STOOD UP, HE
TOOK IT----

Now arrange the circled letters to form the
surprise answer, as suggested by the above
cartoon.

**Print
answer
here**

156

JUMBLE.

Unscramble these four Jumbles, one letter to
each square, to form four ordinary words.

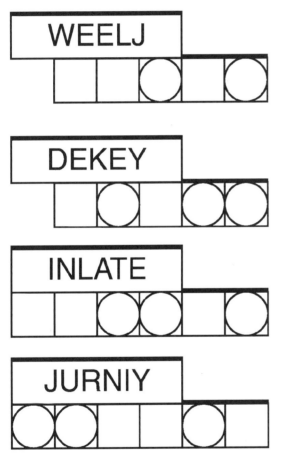

WEELJ

DEKEY

INLATE

JURNIY

I know every inch
of this track

THE VETERAN CON-
DUCTOR BECAME
AN ENGINEER
BECAUSE HE WAS----

Now arrange the circled letters to form the
surprise answer, as suggested by the above
cartoon.

Print answer here

157

JUMBLE®

Unscramble these four Jumbles, one letter to each square, to form four ordinary words.

YAIRN

SEDUE

PONGIE

NISUFE

My old one broke and I have 20 loads today

THE LAUNDRESS RUSHED TO BUY A NEW IRON BECAUSE IT WAS A----

Now arrange the circled letters to form the surprise answer, as suggested by the above cartoon.

Print answer here

" ◯◯◯◯◯◯◯◯ " ◯◯◯◯

JUMBLE®

Unscramble these four Jumbles, one letter to
each square, to form four ordinary words.

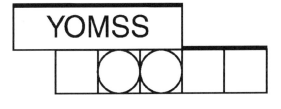

YOMSS

GEESI

HOYLUR

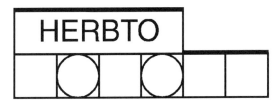

HERBTO

Nothing
else?

Sorry, ma'am,
we're closing

WHAT THE SALES-
MAN GAVE THE
PICKY CUSTOMER.

Now arrange the circled letters to form the
surprise answer, as suggested by the above
cartoon.

Print answer here THE

JUMBLE®

Unscramble these four Jumbles, one letter to
each square, to form four ordinary words.

YOFAR

NABOR

CLANGI

OSOYUJ

Get
busy!

Waiting for the last
batch to get
done, sir

A BAKER CAN GET
AWAY WITH THIS.

Now arrange the circled letters to form the
surprise answer, as suggested by the above
cartoon.

Print
answer
here "◯◯◯◯◯◯" ON THE ◯◯◯

JUMBLE®

Unscramble these four Jumbles, one letter to each square, to form four ordinary words.

YORFT

GITHE

UGUTOD

TENJUK

You're right, sir. Whatever you say, sir

You're my new vice-president

THE YES-MAN WAS PROMOTED BECAUSE HE----

Now arrange the circled letters to form the surprise answer, as suggested by the above cartoon.

Print answer here ◯◯◯ ◯◯◯ "◯◯◯"

JUMBLE®

Unscramble these four Jumbles, one letter to each square, to form four ordinary words.

WORNC

SIFOT

FOTEEF

WOFELL

Don't move. Get those boots off

It's really deep out there

OFTEN FACED BY MOTHERS AFTER A WINTER STORM.

Now arrange the circled letters to form the surprise answer, as suggested by the above cartoon.

Print answer here

A ☐☐☐ ☐☐☐☐ OF ☐☐☐☐

Jet Set JUMBLE®

Challenger Puzzles

JUMBLE®

Unscramble these six Jumbles, one letter to each square, to form six ordinary words.

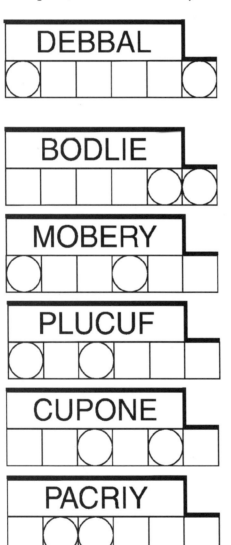

DEBBAL

BODLIE

MOBERY

PLUCUF

CUPONE

PACRIY

Your discounted rate is $5,000

Worth every penny

WHAT SHE PAID FOR A WEEK AT THE DIET SPA.

Now arrange the circled letters to form the surprise answer, as suggested by the above cartoon.

Print answer here

A " ◯◯◯◯◯◯◯ " ◯◯◯◯◯

164

JUMBLE®

Unscramble these six Jumbles, one letter to each square, to form six ordinary words.

GROFTE

GOIBLE

NABYRD

SUMMUE

UIDDEG

CIPEAE

Rex chased him for two miles

WHEN THE SUSPECT WAS CAPTURED, THE CANINE OFFI-CER DESCRIBED IT AS A---

Now arrange the circled letters to form the surprise answer, as suggested by the above cartoon.

Print answer here

" ⬡⬡⬡⬡⬡⬡ " ⬡⬡⬡⬡⬡⬡⬡

JUMBLE.

Unscramble these six Jumbles, one letter to each square, to form six ordinary words.

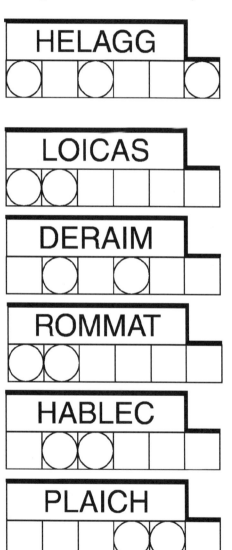

HELAGG

LOICAS

DERAIM

ROMMAT

HABLEC

PLAICH

Nice job. I can see my face in here

WHAT HE CREATED
WHEN HE WAXED
THE PIANO.

Now arrange the circled letters to form the surprise answer, as suggested by the above cartoon.

Print answer here

A " ◯◯◯◯◯◯◯◯◯ " ◯◯◯◯◯

JUMBLE®

Unscramble these six Jumbles, one letter to
each square, to form six ordinary words.

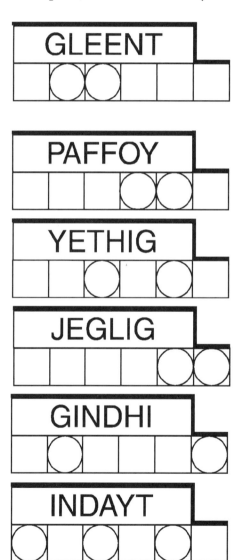

GLEENT

PAFFOY

YETHIG

JEGLIG

GINDHI

INDAYT

En garde

I need to
question
both of
you

WHAT THE DETEC-
TIVE FEARED AT
THE FENCING DUEL.

Now arrange the circled letters to form the
surprise answer, as suggested by the above
cartoon.

Print answer here

JUMBLE®

Unscramble these six Jumbles, one letter to each square, to form six ordinary words.

FACOSI

INPYGA

PREEMA

FLAGDY

TUCSOC

INJOUR

You're doing a fine job, Smitty

Trying my best, boss

OFTEN MADE BY A HARDWORKING PRINTER.

Now arrange the circled letters to form the surprise answer, as suggested by the above cartoon.

Print answer here

A ◯◯◯◯ " ◯◯◯◯◯◯◯◯◯◯ "

JUMBLE

Unscramble these six Jumbles, one letter to
each square, to form six ordinary words.

BIRDHY

FELGUN

VOCONY

SCUMEL

ZEERIF

CATATH

WHEN SHE DECIDED
THE SHOES WERE
TOO EXPENSIVE,
IT WAS----

Now arrange the circled letters to form the
surprise answer, as suggested by the above
cartoon.

Print answer here

" ⃝⃝⃝⃝ " ⃝⃝⃝⃝ ⃝⃝⃝⃝⃝

JUMBLE®

Unscramble these six Jumbles, one letter to each square, to form six ordinary words.

GYRINT

DRIVET

SNAMEA

CEEDIT

SOWDAH

ELCHEK

I want to be successful at my interview

HE WORE AN EXPENSIVE THREE-PIECE SUIT BECAUSE HE HAD A----

Now arrange the circled letters to form the surprise answer, as suggested by the above cartoon.

Print answer here

170

JUMBLE®

Unscramble these six Jumbles, one letter to each square, to form six ordinary words.

CODJUN

HOMAFT

GUSINE

CATNIG

MULEHI

EGWAIH

I use it to seed my fields

THIS INTERESTED THE TAILOR WHEN HE VISITED THE FARM.

Now arrange the circled letters to form the surprise answer, as suggested by the above cartoon.

Print answer here

A " ☐☐☐☐☐☐ " ☐☐☐☐☐☐☐☐

JUMBLE®

Unscramble these six Jumbles, one letter to
each square, to form six ordinary words.

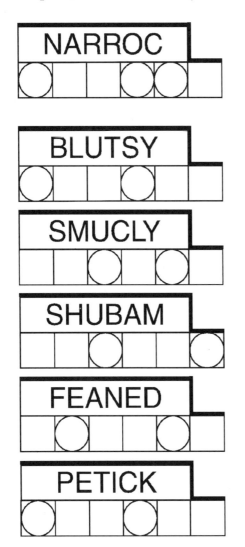

NARROC

BLUTSY

SMUCLY

SHUBAM

FEANED

PETICK

BANK

That's far enough

WHEN THE HUNTER
FOILED THE BANK
ROBBERY, HE
SAID----

Now arrange the circled letters to form the
surprise answer, as suggested by the above
cartoon.

Print answer here

" THE ' ⃝⃝⃝⃝ ' ⃝⃝⃝⃝⃝ ⃝⃝⃝⃝ "

JUMBLE®

Unscramble these six Jumbles, one letter to each square, to form six ordinary words.

TENNIT

SHOOTE

NORMAT

YAQUES

THINEW

TULFAY

LIBRARY

I'm learning how to eat right

It'll help you lose weight

SHE TOOK THE NUTRITION CLASS BECAUSE SHE HAD A---

Now arrange the circled letters to form the surprise answer, as suggested by the above cartoon.

Print answer here

" ◯◯◯◯◯◯◯ " ◯◯◯◯◯◯◯◯◯

JUMBLE®

Unscramble these six Jumbles, one letter to each square, to form six ordinary words.

SLINUM

YATIRR

KNABIG

DOUBIT

HERTAG

RASTIE

Cut it short

No, I want it long

WHAT THE BARBER FACED WHEN DAD AND JUNIOR DISAGREED.

Now arrange the circled letters to form the surprise answer, as suggested by the above cartoon.

Print answer here

A " ◯◯◯◯◯◯ " ◯◯◯◯◯◯◯◯◯◯

JUMBLE®

Unscramble these six Jumbles, one letter to each square, to form six ordinary words.

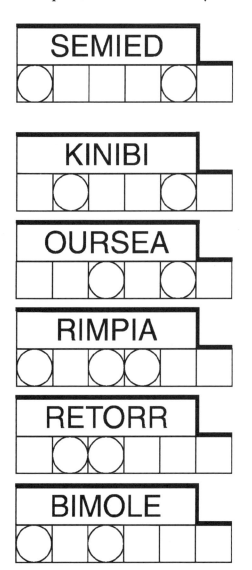

SEMIED

KINIBI

OURSEA

RIMPIA

RETORR

BIMOLE

FRESH CEMENT

Hi, is your daughter in?

Hey, you &$#"**!!!

WHEN THE BLIND DATE ARRIVED, HE MADE A---

Now arrange the circled letters to form the surprise answer, as suggested by the above cartoon.

Print answer here

JUMBLE

Unscramble these six Jumbles, one letter to each square, to form six ordinary words.

TOZALE

GAPOAD

TRULSY

INGRIF

DRUSAB

UNBEAT

She's the maestro's daughter?

HOW SHE GOT THE JOB AS A HARPIST.

Now arrange the circled letters to form the surprise answer, as suggested by the above cartoon.

Print answer here

SHE ⬡⬡⬡⬡⬡⬡ " ⬡⬡⬡⬡⬡⬡ "

JUMBLE®

Unscramble these six Jumbles, one letter to
each square, to form six ordinary words.

LAWESE

ROGERF

LAYSIE

LETTAC

BENZAR

PHATAY

Left full rudder.
All ahead two-
thirds

Aye
aye,
sir

WHEN THE JUNIOR
OFFICER MANNED
THE BRIDGE, HE
BECAME THE----

Now arrange the circled letters to form the
surprise answer, as suggested by the above
cartoon.

Print answer here

Unscramble these six Jumbles, one letter to
each square, to form six ordinary words.

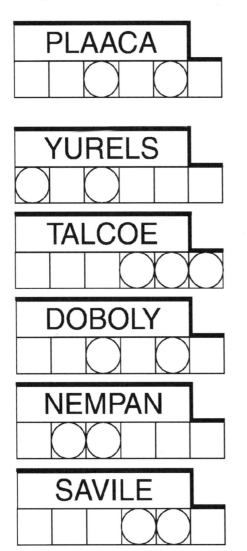

PLAACA

YURELS

TALCOE

DOBOLY

NEMPAN

SAVILE

Iron the clothes
for the kids and
start dinner, George

Yes,
dear

WHEN SHE HAD A
LAST-MINUTE
BUSINESS MEETING,
HE WAS---

Now arrange the circled letters to form the
surprise answer, as suggested by the above
cartoon.

Print answer here

" ⬡⬡⬡⬡⬡⬡⬡ " INTO ⬡⬡⬡⬡⬡⬡

JUMBLE®

Unscramble these six Jumbles, one letter to each square, to form six ordinary words.

CYRIKT

PLUBAR

DRIFOL

CAFFEE

YARVOS

NOTAIR

How 'bout the contract?

Paragraph 15 needs work

WHAT THEY DID WHEN THE EXOTIC DANCER APPEARED ON STAGE.

Now arrange the circled letters to form the surprise answer, as suggested by the above cartoon.

Print answer here

" ◯◯◯◯◯◯ " ◯◯◯◯◯◯◯

JUMBLE®

Unscramble these six Jumbles, one letter to
each square, to form six ordinary words.

YEASUN

BOICED

WHAREK

KLEACT

CLOTUC

GRAYUS

Ouch! I'm all
scratched up

WHAT THE HIKER
EXPERIENCED WHEN
SHE FELL INTO
THE BRAMBLE
BUSH.

Now arrange the circled letters to form the
surprise answer, as suggested by the above
cartoon.

Print answer here

" ⬡⬡⬡⬡⬡⬡⬡ " ⬡⬡⬡⬡⬡

JUMBLE®

Unscramble these six Jumbles, one letter to each square, to form six ordinary words.

TIPPUL

SLIMIE

MINTEY

FLUGAR

FRAIDT

BIDITT

...and in appreciation I present you with this gold...

He's the best

WHAT THE OUT-STANDING TAILOR RECEIVED AT HIS RETIREMENT PARTY.

Now arrange the circled letters to form the surprise answer, as suggested by the above cartoon.

Print answer here

A " ⬡⬡⬡⬡⬡⬡⬡ " ⬡⬡⬡⬡⬡⬡⬡⬡

JUMBLE

Unscramble these six Jumbles, one letter to
each square, to form six ordinary words.

CLOUNK

TAJUNY

ENERGE

GLUEED

HYNWIN

LIRMAN

Either he helps
around the house
or I go
on strike

But
dear…

THE LABOR
LEADER AND HIS
WIFE WENT TO THE
MARRIAGE COUN-
SELOR FOR---

Now arrange the circled letters to form the
surprise answer, as suggested by the above
cartoon.

Print answer here

A "◯◯◯◯◯" ◯◯◯◯◯◯◯

JUMBLE®

Unscramble these six Jumbles, one letter to
each square, to form six ordinary words.

RATTAR

NAHLED

BOLUDE

DAYMAL

CONNAY

SOLANG

TEN HUT!

I'm too tired after that long march

WHY THE SOLDIER
SAT DOWN WHEN
THE SERGEANT
CALLED,
"ATTENTION!"

Now arrange the circled letters to form the
surprise answer, as suggested by the above
cartoon.

Print answer here

HE ⬡⬡⬡⬡⬡ ' ⬡ " ⬡⬡⬡⬡⬡ " IT

Answers

1. **Jumbles:** HYENA ELOPE GOLFER DULCET
   Answer: What the swimmers took when they got married—THE "PLUNGE"

2. **Jumbles:** ACUTE PANDA MEMORY SOCKET
   Answer: What the obnoxious actress did on the set—MADE A "SCENE"

3. **Jumbles:** FAINT BRAIN RAREFY TROUGH
   Answer: Where Mom put dinner when she got home late—ON THE FRONT BURNER

4. **Jumbles:** BUXOM HAIRY JOBBER ZENITH
   Answer: What the nondenominational choir produced—"HARMONY"

5. **Jumbles:** MOUTH FANCY TRUDGE COSTLY
   Answer: The accountant bought a new calculator so he—COULD "COUNT" ON IT

6. **Jumbles:** DOGMA CHIDE TONGUE FEWEST
   Answer: What the chicken farmer did to his workers—"EGGED" THEM ON

7. **Jumbles:** CRIME FROZE EVOLVE DAWNED
   Answer: When Grandpa bought gumballs, they were—A DIME A DOZEN

8. **Jumbles:** SKULK DUCAT FONDLY DEFACE
   Answer: What the weatherman gave the listeners—THE "COLD" FACTS

9. **Jumbles:** SOGGY FRUIT CUDDLE BEGONE
   Answer: When the woman spotted the handsome bachelor, he was—"SINGLED" OUT

10. **Jumbles:** HOUSE BOOTH THIRTY GUZZLE
    Answer: When the golfer ended up in the tall grass, he said, "This is—A ROUGH SHOT"

11. **Jumbles:** DOILY HIKER GALAXY INLAND
    Answer: When the kids wanted a ride in the wagon, Dad—"HANDLED" IT

12. **Jumbles:** AFOOT GAUDY BUZZER LACKEY
    Answer: What a "large" change made the king—"REGAL"

13. **Jumbles:** TOPAZ VIPER CORNER FRIGID
    Answer: What she won at the raffle—THE "GRAND" PRIZE

14. **Jumbles:** TROTH PANSY BEFOUL SCURVY
    Answer: Experienced by the chef when the diners returned the meals—A SOUR TASTE

15. **Jumbles:** REBEL FETCH JOYFUL SALUTE
    Answer: What she gave the artist on the prowl—THE BRUSH-OFF

16. **Jumbles:** DROOP FEIGN BRIDGE POCKET
    Answer: The banjo player selected the new car because he was—GOOD AT "PICKING"

17. **Jumbles:** FORCE CASTE MALICE VERMIN
    Answer: What he flew when he got his pilot's license—"COMMERCIAL"

18. **Jumbles:** WHISK SEIZE WATERY BLOUSE
    Answer: When she made her own dress, Mom said it was—SEW SEW

19. **Jumbles:** LLAMA BEGUN LAGOON IMMUNE
    Answer: How he described his fireworks business—"BOOMING"

20. **Jumbles:** MAKER BURST PEWTER KNOTTY
    Answer: What the interrogator experienced when the faucet dripped all night—WATER TORTURE

21. **Jumbles:** BLOOD FAIRY MARVEL SLEEPY
    Answer: When the poetry student's work improved, she went from—BAD TO "VERSE"

22. **Jumbles:** AVAIL VISOR BECOME POLICY
    Answer: What the shady golfer tried to do—IMPROVE HIS "LIE"

23. **Jumbles:** JOLLY WHOSE ASTRAY INWARD
    Answer: When the skinny guy won the eating contest, his competitors found it—HARD TO "SWALLOW"

24. **Jumbles:** GAILY EMERY LAWFUL MAINLY
    Answer: What she got from the college jock in the laundry room—A "WRING"

25. **Jumbles:** WALTZ EVENT PARDON SPORTY
    Answer: She spurned the printer's advances because he—WASN'T HER "TYPE"

26. **Jumbles:** CREEK LYRIC UNHOLY BEHEAD
    Answer: What she was left with when her hair came out the wrong color—A HUE AND A CRY

27. **Jumbles:** REARM MERGE MULISH CAMPUS
    Answer: The forecaster described the heat wave as—A SUMMER SIMMER

28. **Jumbles:** DALLY SCARF PLACID BEHOLD
    Answer: The only time of year the crowd wanted the star shortstop to do this—DROP THE "BALL"

29. **Jumbles:** TASTY VITAL TWINGE ORCHID
    Answer: What it takes to make a fast meal—LOTS OF "THAWED"

30. **Jumbles:** DAILY WHEEL POLICE MISUSE
    Answer: Why the mogul didn't pay the sculptor for the bust—HE WAS "CHISELED"

31. **Jumbles:** GUMBO FUNNY BANNER RADIUM
    Answer: What the angry driver used to pay his speeding fine—"MAD" MONEY

32. **Jumbles:** METAL AUGUR FOSSIL APPALL
    Answer: Why the fireman woke before dawn on his day off—A FALSE "ALARM"

33. **Jumbles:** UNWED FLORA UPLIFT BANTER
    Answer: The furniture salesman was hired because he was—TOP "DRAWER"

34. **Jumbles:** JULEP PATIO BUSHEL TOUCHY
    Answer: How she felt when her cobbler recipe won the blue ribbon—JUST "PEACHY"

35. **Jumbles:** BISON SWISH INNATE BLUING
    Answer: When the kitchen help fell behind, the chef was—"STEWING"

36. **Jumbles:** LADLE HOBBY MOSAIC BODILY
    Answer: Hard to raise after spring planting—HIS BODY

37. **Jumbles:** RUSTY TRIPE SUPERB FALLOW
    Answer: When her purse was snatched, the turnpike oasis became a—"WREST" STOP

38. **Jumbles:** DINER CUBIC AMOEBA CHROME
    Answer: What the barber did on vacation—"COMBED" THE BEACH

39. **Jumbles:** OCCUR BLESS UNLESS VARIED
    Answer: When the retiree returned to college, he was placed in the—"SENIOR" CLASS

40. **Jumbles:** OXIDE CEASE PURVEY DEVOUR
    Answer: What the photographer feared when she shopped for a swimsuit—OVEREXPOSURE

41. **Jumbles:** PIECE MINUS NOUGAT BANISH
    Answer: This can curl your hair at a beauty salon—GOSSIP

42. **Jumbles:** TRUTH EXILE HIEFER PROFIT
    Answer: In what inning did they pass the bottle around?—THE "FIFTH"

43. **Jumbles:** MESSY PARKA LIQUOR NAUSEA
    Answer: A round belly can be the result of too many—SQUARE MEALS

44. **Jumbles:** NERVY QUEEN REFUGE DAMASK
    Answer: What she told the baker to do on her birthday cake—"FUDGE" THE YEARS

45. **Jumbles:** FEWER HEAVY STURDY EFFIGY
    Answer: She went away to college in a new car because she—WAS "GIFTED"

46. **Jumbles:** CRUSH EVOKE RABBIT PEOPLE
    Answer: When he bought the jalopy, he ended up with a—"HEAP" OF TROUBLE

47. **Jumbles:** POKED INEPT LUNACY FIESTA
Answer: An indifferent student can do this in astronomy class—TAKE UP "SPACE"

48. **Jumbles:** ROBOT LIGHT PODIUM GLOOMY
Answer: What the fast-talking mechanic seemed to be—A "MOTOR" MOUTH

49. **Jumbles:** LINGO TEPID EMERGE CURFEW
Answer: Why he didn't join the glacier expedition—HE GOT "COLD" FEET

50. **Jumbles:** LEGAL PAGAN INLAID AERATE
Answer: The bald-headed friends had a difficult time doing this—"PARTING"

51. **Jumbles:** WINCE HEDGE REBUKE COERCE
Answer: Knitted with a complex stitch—HER BROW

52. **Jumbles:** CYCLE LARVA KINDLY BANGLE
Answer: After an hour-long battle with the marlin, the fisherman was—"REELING"

53. **Jumbles:** AGLOW GLADE AMAZON DONKEY
Answer: What he ended up with when he ate all the doughnuts—A "GLAZED" LOOK

54. **Jumbles:** CHAIR TULLE FLURRY PURITY
Answer: What the surgeon turned into at the annual roast—A REAL CUTUP

55. **Jumbles:** PUPIL UNITY TANGLE HERESY
Answer: One too many made him do this—SLEEP "TIGHT"

56. **Jumbles:** SINGE CABIN UPSHOT RADIUS
Answer: What the deep-voiced guy turned into when he joined the prison quartet—A STRIPED "BASS"

57. **Jumbles:** PRINT BEFOG GAMBLE ERMINE
Answer: Why the window washer took a break—FOR "PANE" RELIEF

58. **Jumbles:** ELITE APART INFECT SICKEN
Answer: Often running around a backyard—A PICKET FENCE

59. **Jumbles:** ENACT DAISY GARISH KITTEN
Answer: What Mom faced when she forgot to thaw dinner—"ICY" STARES

60. **Jumbles:** BULGY ITCHY VELVET UNLOAD
Answer: Why the operator went to work despite a heavy cold—THE "CALL" TO DUTY

61. **Jumbles:** SNARL BOWER LAXITY EXOTIC
Answer: What an expensive meal can cost—A LOT OF CALORIES

62. **Jumbles:** GUMMY TAFFY OCELOT GROTTO
Answer: When he ordered one for the road, he—GOT A CAR

63. **Jumbles:** DUCHY GUESS MOTHER BANDIT
Answer: What Junior did to Dad at the pet shop—"HOUNDED" HIM

64. **Jumbles:** ROUSE FRAUD PELVIS SALOON
Answer: Why the sweet shop went out of business—SALES "SOURED"

65. **Jumbles:** ALIVE SAVOR BLITHE KNIGHT
Answer: Many will do this on Valentine's Day—TAKE IT TO "HEART"

66. **Jumbles:** NUDGE DOWNY POTENT ANYWAY
Answer: What the children did when Mom brought home cookies—"PUT THEM AWAY"

67. **Jumbles:** ARDOR MIRTH JOCKEY RANCID
Answer: When the knight made a snide remark, it resulted in a—"CRACK" IN HIS ARMOR

68. **Jumbles:** STUNG WEIGH FEDORA OMELET
Answer: What the shepherd did when the mother and lambs strayed from the flock—MADE A EWE TURN

69. **Jumbles:** MUSTY SNOWY ABACUS BEAUTY
Answer: He destroyed the piece of sculpture because the—BUST WAS A BUST

70. **Jumbles:** TRYST JERKY BICKER VALUED
Answer: "Aides" can give you this—IDEAS

71. **Jumbles:** FLAME YOKEL EULOGY FROTHY
Answer: What the farmer gave the hired hands—A "LOFTY" GOAL

72. **Jumbles:** CRACK LOWLY SMOKER UPROAR
Answer: When the tailor made a suit for the mobster, he said it was—"SEAMY" WORK

73. **Jumbles:** RIVET MANGY FEEBLE AIRWAY
Answer: When they vacationed on the posh island, they were surrounded by—WATER

74. **Jumbles:** FILMY TOXIC VIOLIN EXPEND
Answer: What the bookie gave the waiter—A NICE "TIP"

75. **Jumbles:** TARDY ANKLE SEETHE DEVICE
Answer: How the steamy soap opera star left the fans—IN A "LATHER"

76. **Jumbles:** GIVEN CARGO DAHLIA CLERGY
Answer: What the detectives did when they spotted the credit-card thieves—"CHARGED"

77. **Jumbles:** USURY DOUBT WINTRY MISFIT
Answer: When touring Germany, the ulcer sufferer took a—TURN FOR THE "WURST"

78. **Jumbles:** BOUND PROXY ANGINA REDUCE
Answer: How long did the challenger last against the champ?—AROUND A ROUND

79. **Jumbles:** AIDED PLAID WEAKEN AUTHOR
Answer: What the tipsy gambler and the dice had in common—THEY WERE "LOADED"

80. **Jumbles:** IDIOT FINIS QUAVER PUSHER
Answer: What the kids faced after dinner—A "DISH-PUTE"

81. **Jumbles:** POACH AFTER JUSTLY BELLOW
Answer: What the trainer gave the greyhound during his morning workout—A FEW "LAPS"

82. **Jumbles:** SCARY BRINY PAUPER THRASH
Answer: When the robber was caught on the steps, the cops said it was—A STAIR "CASE"

83. **Jumbles:** HASTY BELIE STRONG FUTURE
Answer: What the king experienced when he was awakened by the protesters—A STATE OF "UNREST"

84. **Jumbles:** QUAIL JUDGE PETITE CHALET
Answer: Known to leave when teenagers have their friends over—PEACE AND QUIET

85. **Jumbles:** RAVEN COVEY GULLET YEARLY
Answer: What it took to sandbag the town against the rising river—A LEVEE LEVY

86. **Jumbles:** AGILE BLIMP IMPEND LIMPID
Answer: He didn't take sides in the debate because he was a—"MIDDLE" MAN

87. **Jumbles:** TOXIN FOYER MORBID ENOUGH
Answer: When the judge presided over the long trial, he—FOUND IT "TRYING"

88. **Jumbles:** NOVEL IMBUE WOEFUL MOTIVE
Answer: What they needed to listen to the book on tape—VOLUME VOLUME

89. **Jumbles:** BROOK COLON FABRIC UTMOST
Answer: Where the band ended up when their concert fizzled—AT "ROCK" BOTTOM

90. **Jumbles:** GUILT ORBIT FUNGUS TANKER
Answer: When the king went out for the night, he wore his—"REIGN" OUTFIT

91. **Jumbles:** GORGE FOCUS DECENT RAGLAN
Answer: Why the robbers headed for the seashore—THE COAST WAS "CLEAR"

92. **Jumbles:** TITLE SOOTY FLATLY POISON
Answer: The jockey's mail didn't arrive because it was—LEFT AT THE "POST"

93. **Jumbles:** ABBOT STEED HORROR FROZEN
Answer: How the drunken cowboy felt when the sheriff put him in the cooler—NOT SO HOT

94. **Jumbles:** BEFIT PHONY QUIVER FABLED
Answer: When the judge had an early court call, he found defendants—UP BEFORE HIM

95. **Jumbles:** OLDER TWEAK FAMISH EFFORT
Answer: Why the door-to-door salesman was spurned—HE "ASKED" FOR IT

185

96. **Jumbles:** COUGH YACHT KIDNAP NEWEST
Answer: When she got the bill for the diamond pin, he got—"STUCK" WITH IT

97. **Jumbles:** KITTY LATCH CHOSEN LANCER
Answer: What he discovered when he tried to open the latch—THERE'S A CATCH

98. **Jumbles:** RAPID TUNED GAMBIT CENSUS
Answer: The professor skipped class on a balmy day because he was—"ABSENT" MINDED

99. **Jumbles:** YODEL CLOAK AROUND PUZZLE
Answer: How the locksmith felt on a busy day— ALL "KEYED" UP

100. **Jumbles:** DERBY FETID COOKIE GUILTY
Answer: Although he was a vegetarian, the diner had a—"BEEFY" LOOK

101. **Jumbles:** NOISE FACET INHALE FIGURE
Answer: When the boss gave her a pat on the shoulder, she found it—"TOUCHING"

102. **Jumbles:** KNOWN HUMAN OSSIFY BESIDE
Answer: What she got when he took her shopping— HIS MONEY

103. **Jumbles:** EXTOL ARMOR VANISH DEBTOR
Answer: When her hair returned to its natural color, she went back to—HER ROOTS

104. **Jumbles:** VIGIL LYING CORPSE THWART
Answer: What a seven-foot center can be to a basketball team—"PIVOT-AL"

105. **Jumbles:** PUDGY ERUPT MALLET JESTER
Answer: When they settled their disagreement over a new bed, they—PUT IT TO "REST"

106. **Jumbles:** BASSO TRAIT INCOME ADAGIO
Answer: The exotic dancer quit because her paycheck was—TOO "MODEST"

107. **Jumbles:** PROBE AGING JUMBLE BOUGHT
Answer: What the drivers did in the demolition derby— A "BANG-UP" JOB

108. **Jumbles:** LILAC PAYEE SINFUL BROOCH
Answer: Why the blond newscaster moderated the debate—SHE WAS "FAIR"

109. **Jumbles:** WHILE DEITY VISION BEHALF
Answer: What the librarian did to the remodeling plan— "SHELVED" IT

110. **Jumbles:** BOUGH CRAZE DISCUS WEAPON
Answer: After hitting the showers, the aging pitcher was— "WASHED" UP

111. **Jumbles:** PLUSH GUISE BEHAVE CYMBAL
Answer: What he ended up with when he paid good money to lose weight—LESS OF EACH

112. **Jumbles:** CAMEO SHEEP BETRAY HARDLY
Answer: When the best-selling biography became a movie, it turned into—THE "REEL" STORY

113. **Jumbles:** GLOAT WEDGE BAUBLE EXEMPT
Answer: The running-shoe company hired the sprinter to—GET A LEG UP

114. **Jumbles:** FEVER BROOD ENTIRE MILDEW
Answer: When the illegally parked cars blocked traffic, the cop—TOWED THE LINE

115. **Jumbles:** TWINE DOWDY QUORUM TURKEY
Answer: Why he couldn't go to the dinner party in his favorite shirt—IT WAS "WORN" OUT

116. **Jumbles:** LURID MINOR MANAGE CASKET
Answer: When the gangster got a tattoo, he became a—"MARKED" MAN

117. **Jumbles:** SANDY SORRY REVERE BUOYED
Answer: Where Mom took her toddler when she went shopping—TO THE "NURSERY"

118. **Jumbles:** HITCH CHALK EXCISE TUXEDO
Answer: What the angry witch gave the tax collector— A "HEX" HIKE

119. **Jumbles:** MOURN CYNIC TREATY RENDER
Answer: What the bass fiddler found tough to do— CARRY A TUNE

120. **Jumbles:** SMOKY TRILL DEMURE EMBALM
Answer: This was brewing at the beer maker—"TROUBLE"

121. **Jumbles:** AWFUL MAGIC LOTION BAZAAR
Answer: When the policeman bought a new uniform, the tailor altered the—LONG ARM OF THE LAW

122. **Jumbles:** WHINE LOFTY INVADE AWHILE
Answer: What happened to his ski vacation after he took a spill—IT WENT "DOWNHILL"

123. **Jumbles:** CROAK PENCE DECADE KENNEL
Answer: When the window came down on him, he said it was a—"PANE" IN THE NECK

124. **Jumbles:** CABLE MERCY NAUGHT DEBATE
Answer: What city cops seek to do with speeding motorists—"CURB" THEM

125. **Jumbles:** FENCE MILKY PONCHO IMBIBE
Answer: Where she ended up when the cucumber crop was harvested—IN A "PICKLE"

126. **Jumbles:** BRASS LITHE NEEDLE GRATIS
Answer: What cowboys do on the range—STEER STEER

127. **Jumbles:** JOKER INLET ABOUND STOLID
Answer: Spending hours looking through a telescope gave the astronomer a—"DISTANT" LOOK

128. **Jumbles:** FLAUT HOARD SINGLE BARIUM
Answer: Why the bride didn't want a train on her wedding gown—IT'S A "DRAG"

129. **Jumbles:** TARRY YOUTH ALWAYS BEWARE
Answer: She kept the hand-me-down chest because it was—A "TREASURE"

130. **Jumbles:** FABLE ONION CRAVAT POETIC
Answer: What they used to join the in-crowd at the hot dance club—THE ENTRANCE

131. **Jumbles:** GRIPE BRAWL PARITY SPEEDY
Answer: The thief was arrested because the credit card was—"SWIPED"

132. **Jumbles:** GUIDE JUROR BARREL REALTY
Answer: What the henpecked king considered his wife— THE RULER RULER

133. **Jumbles:** BALMY SPURN SNAPPY BEDBUG
Answer: The bank manager rose to the top because he was—ON THE UP AND UP

134. **Jumbles:** TACKY DUSKY TOWARD CATCHY
Answer: What the blonde experienced when she became a brunette—HER "DARK" DAYS

135. **Jumbles:** VILLA LINER SCHEME ORATOR
Answer: How the soldier felt at roll call—ILL AT EASE

136. **Jumbles:** WIPED ERASE ATOMIC SCORCH
Answer: When the thoroughbred broke out in a rash, he was—"SCRATCHED"

137. **Jumbles:** GASSY EMPTY PONDER SLEIGH
Answer: What the editor and the tailor shared in their daily routine—GOING TO "PRESS"

138. **Jumbles:** TESTY BATHE BUMPER RECTOR
Answer: When the spy wore a wig, it was—"TOP" SECRET

139. **Jumbles:** ESSAY HELLO NETHER RELISH
Answer: What the animal trainer was paid for his circus act—THE LION'S SHARE

140. **Jumbles:** DRAFT EXULT BEHIND BUTTER
Answer: When the rival "sweet" shops had a price war, they ended up in a—"BITTER" BATTLE

141. **Jumbles:** CAPON EJECT FINISH DEFINE
Answer: Sent to the showers, the hurler remained— OFF "PITCH"

142. **Jumbles:** NAÏVE YEARN COUSIN STODGY
Answer: When reveille was sounded, the commander said it was a—"ROUSING" EVENT

143. **Jumbles:** WAFER GNARL MADMAN LEEWAY
Answer: What his buddies gave him when he took up knitting—THE "NEEDLE"

144. **Jumbles:** NOBLE DELVE OPPOSE BOLERO
Answer: When the submarine reached periscope depth, it was—AT "SEE" LEVEL

145. **Jumbles:** MADLY FISHY SWERVE HYMNAL
Answer: How the seamstress felt before the big dance—"HEMMED" IN

146. **Jumbles:** BEGOT OWING FORKED BROKER
Answer: Why the student rock band didn't play at the party before finals—THEY WERE "BOOKED"

147. **Jumbles:** WRATH ELUDE POORLY CABANA
Answer: What the customer got when his steak was undercooked—A "RAW" DEAL

148. **Jumbles:** KINKY BAGGY VICUNA PLURAL
Answer: All the lights on in the house left Dad—"GLARING"

149. **Jumbles:** CLOTH LIVEN MEADOW GARBLE
Answer: When the bowler was filmed for the ad, he became a—"ROLL" MODEL

150. **Jumbles:** HONEY FAITH KOSHER WIDEST
Answer: What the furniture maker wanted to do before he went home—"FINISH" HIS WORK

151. **Jumbles:** DRONE BRAVO GROUCH PENCIL
Answer: What the investigator decided to do after working all day—GO UNDERCOVER

152. **Jumbles:** ROBIN TABOO DROWSY SUBWAY
Answer: Turns up at the end of a dynasty—THE WORD "NASTY"

153. **Jumbles:** DOUGH TIGER AGHAST HALVED
Answer: The farmer let his son keep the pet kid because he didn't want to—GET HIS GOAT

154. **Jumbles:** TWEET STAID FACING INTONE
Answer: When he was stood up, he took it—SITTING DOWN

155. **Jumbles:** JEWEL KEYED ENTAIL INJURY
Answer: The veteran conductor became an engineer because he was—WELL "TRAINED"

156. **Jumbles:** RAINY SUEDE PIGEON INFUSE
Answer: The laundress rushed to buy a new iron because it was a—"PRESSING" NEED

157. **Jumbles:** MOSSY SIEGE HOURLY BOTHER
Answer: What the salesman gave the picky customer—THE SHOE SHOO

158. **Jumbles:** FORAY BARON LACING JOYOUS
Answer: What the henpecked king considered his wife—"LOAFING" ON THE JOB

159. **Jumbles:** FORTY EIGHT DUGOUT JUNKET
Answer: The yes-man was promoted because he—GOT THE "NOD"

160. **Jumbles:** CROWN FOIST TOFFEE FELLOW
Answer: Often faced by mothers after a winter storm—A FEW FEET OF SNOW

161. **Jumbles:** DABBLE BOILED EMBRYO CUPFUL POUNCE PIRACY
Answer: What she paid for a week at the diet spa—A "REDUCED" PRICE

162. **Jumbles:** FORGET OBLIGE BRANDY MUSEUM GUIDED APIECE
Answer: When the suspect was captured, the canine officer described it as a—"DOGGED" PURSUIT

163. **Jumbles:** HAGGLE SOCIAL ADMIRE MARMOT BLEACH CALIPH
Answer: What he created when he waxed the piano—A "POLISHED" IMAGE

164. **Jumbles:** GENTLE PAYOFF EIGHTY JIGGLE HIDING DAINTY
Answer: What the detective feared at the fencing duel—GETTING "FOILED"

165. **Jumbles:** FIASCO PAYING AMPERE GADFLY STUCCO JUNIOR
Answer: Often made by a hardworking printer—A GOOD "IMPRESSION"

166. **Jumbles:** HYBRID ENGULF CONVOY MUSCLE FRIEZE ATTACH
Answer: When she decided the shoes were too expensive, it was—"HEAD" OVER HEELS

167. **Jumbles:** TRYING DIVERT SEAMAN DECEIT SHADOW HECKLE
Answer: He wore an expensive three-piece suit because he had a—"VESTED" INTEREST

168. **Jumbles:** JOCUND FATHOM GENIUS ACTING HELIUM AWEIGH
Answer: This interested the tailor when he visited the farm—A "SOWING" MACHINE

169. **Jumbles:** RANCOR SUBTLY CLUMSY AMBUSH DEAFEN PICKET
Answer: When the hunter foiled the bank robbery, he said—"THE 'BUCK' STOPS HERE"

170. **Jumbles:** INTENT SOOTHE MATRON QUEASY WHITEN FAULTY
Answer: She took the nutrition class because she had a—"HEALTHY" INTEREST

171. **Jumbles:** MUSLIN RARITY BAKING OUTBID GATHER SATIRE
Answer: What the barber faced when Dad and Junior disagreed—A "HAIRY" SITUATION

172. **Jumbles:** DEMISE BIKINI AROUSE IMPAIR TERROR MOBILE
Answer: When the blind date arrived, he made a—BAD "IMPRESSION"

173. **Jumbles:** ZEALOT PAGODA SULTRY FIRING ABSURD BUTANE
Answer: How she got the job as a harpist—SHE PULLED "STRINGS"

174. **Jumbles:** WEASEL FORGER EASILY CATTLE BRAZEN APATHY
Answer: When the junior officer manned the bridge, he became the—STEERING "WHEEL"

175. **Jumbles:** ALPACA SURELY LOCATE BLOODY PENMAN VALISE
Answer: When she had a last-minute business meeting, he was—"PRESSED" INTO ACTION

176. **Jumbles:** TRICKY BURLAP FLORID EFFACE SAVORY RATION
Answer: What they did when the exotic dancer appeared on stage—"BARELY" NOTICED

177. **Jumbles:** UNEASY BODICE HAWKER TACKLE OCCULT SUGARY
Answer: What the hiker experienced when she fell into the bramble bush—"STICKER" SHOCK

178. **Jumbles:** PULPIT SIMILE ENMITY FRUGAL ADRIFT TIDBIT
Answer: What the outstanding tailor received at his retirement party—A "FITTING" TRIBUTE

179. **Jumbles:** UNLOCK JAUNTY RENEGE DELUGE WHINNY MARLIN
Answer: The labor leader and his wife went to the marriage counselor for—A "UNION" MEETING

180. **Jumbles:** TARTAR HANDLE DOUBLE MALADY CANYON SLOGAN
Answer: Why the soldier sat down when the sergeant called, "Attention!"—HE COULDN'T "STAND" IT

Need More Jumbles®?

Jumble® Books

More than 175 puzzles each!

Jammin' Jumble®
$9.95 • ISBN: 1-57243-844-4

Jazzy Jumble®
$9.95 • ISBN: 978-1-57243-962-7

Jet Set Jumble®
$9.95 • ISBN: 978-1-60078-353-1

Joyful Jumble®
$9.95 • ISBN: 978-1-60078-079-0

Juke Joint Jumble®
$9.95 • ISBN: 978-1-60078-295-4

Jumble® at Work
$9.95 • ISBN: 1-57243-147-4

Jumble® Celebration
$9.95 • ISBN: 978-1-60078-134-6

Jumble® Explosion
$9.95 • ISBN: 978-1-60078-078-3

Jumble® Fever
$9.95 • ISBN: 1-57243-593-3

Jumble® Fiesta
$9.95 • ISBN: 1-57243-626-3

Jumble® Fun
$9.95 • ISBN: 1-57243-379-5

Jumble® Madness
$9.95 • ISBN: 1-892049-24-4

Jumble® Mania
$9.95 • ISBN: 1-57243-697-2

Jumble® See & Search
$9.95 • ISBN: 1-57243-549-6

Jumble® See & Search 2
$9.95 • ISBN: 1-57243-734-0

Jumble® Surprise
$9.95 • ISBN: 1-57243-320-5

Jumpin' Jumble®
$9.95 • ISBN: 978-1-60078-027-1

Rainy Day Jumble®
$9.95 • ISBN: 978-1-60078-352-4

Ready, Set, Jumble®
$9.95 • ISBN: 978-1-60078-133-0

Sports Jumble®
$9.95 • ISBN: 1-57243-113-X

Summer Fun Jumble®
$9.95 • ISBN: 1-57243-114-8

Travel Jumble®
$9.95 • ISBN: 1-57243-198-9

TV Jumble®
$9.95 • ISBN: 1-57243-461-9

Jumble® Genius
$9.95 • ISBN: 1-57243-896-7

Jumble® Grab Bag
$9.95 • ISBN: 1-57243-273-X

Jumble® Jackpot
$9.95 • ISBN: 1-57243-897-5

Jumble® Jambalaya
$9.95 • ISBN: 978-1-60078-294-7

Jumble® Jamboree
$9.95 • ISBN: 1-57243-696-4

Jumble® Jubilee
$9.95 • ISBN: 1-57243-231-4

Jumble® Juggernaut
$9.95 • ISBN: 978-1-60078-026-4

Jumble® Junction
$9.95 • ISBN: 1-57243-380-9

Jumble® Jungle
$9.95 • ISBN: 978-1-57243-961-0

Oversize Jumble® Books

More than 500 puzzles each!

Generous Jumble®
$19.95 • ISBN: 1-57243-385-X

Giant Jumble®
$19.95 • ISBN: 1-57243-349-3

Gigantic Jumble®
$19.95 • ISBN: 1-57243-426-0

Jumbo Jumble®
$19.95 • ISBN: 1-57243-314-0

The Very Best of Jumble® BrainBusters
$19.95 • ISBN: 1-57243-845-2

Jumble® Crosswords™

More than 175 puzzles each!

More Jumble® Crosswords™
$9.95 • ISBN: 1-57243-386-8

Jumble® Crosswords™ Jackpot
$9.95 • ISBN: 1-57243-615-8

Jumble® Crosswords™ Jamboree
$9.95 • ISBN: 1-57243-787-1

Jumble® BrainBusters™

More than 175 puzzles each!

Jumble® BrainBusters™
$9.95 • ISBN: 1-892049-28-7

Jumble® BrainBusters™ II
$9.95 • ISBN: 1-57243-424-4

Jumble® BrainBusters™ III
$9.95 • ISBN: 1-57243-463-5

Jumble® BrainBusters™ IV
$9.95 • ISBN: 1-57243-489-9

Jumble® BrainBusters™ 5
$9.95 • ISBN: 1-57243-548-8

Jumble® BrainBusters™ Bonanza
$9.95 • ISBN: 1-57243-616-6

Boggle™ BrainBusters™
$9.95 • ISBN: 1-57243-592-5

Boggle™ BrainBusters™ 2
$9.95 • ISBN: 1-57243-788-X

Jumble® BrainBusters™ Junior
$9.95 • ISBN: 1-892049-29-5

Jumble® BrainBusters™ Junior II
$9.95 • ISBN: 1-57243-425-2

Fun in the Sun with Jumble® BrainBusters™
$9.95 • ISBN: 1-57243-733-2